D0841974

COULD YOU EVER BECOME A CATHOLIC PRIEST?

Could You Ever Become a Catholic Priest?

Christopher J. Duquin and
Lorene Hanley Duquin

Afterword by Paul S. Loverde, STL, JCL
Bishop of Ogdensburg

ALBA·HOUSE alba house NEW·YORK

SOCIETY OF ST. PAUL, 2187 VICTORY BLVD., STATEN ISLAND, NEW YORK 10314

ST PAULS

Library of Congress Cataloging-in-Publication Data

Duquin, Christopher J.
   Could you ever become a Catholic priest? / Christopher J. Duquin,
Lorene Hanley Duquin.
      p.   cm.
   Includes bibliographical references.
   ISBN 0-8189-0816-5
   1. Vocation, Ecclesiastical.   I. Duquin, Lorene Hanley.
II. Title
BX2380.D87   1998
248.8'92—dc21   98-13335
                                        CIP

Produced and designed in the United States of America by the
Fathers and Brothers of the Society of St. Paul,
2187 Victory Boulevard, Staten Island, New York 10314,
as part of their communications apostolate.

ISBN: 0-8189-0816-5

Printing Information:

Current Printing - first digit   1   2   3   4   5   6   7   8   9   10

Year of Current Printing - first year shown

1998   1999   2000   2001   2002   2003   2004   2005

This book is dedicated to the Memory of
Father David Kirsch
whose priesthood is my inspiration.
He was the first person to ask me the question,
"Could you ever become a Catholic priest?"
Christopher J. Duquin

Table of Contents

Acknowledgments

This book is about the Lord, who calls us, and the stories we share about that call. This book would not have been possible without the priests, seminarians and men discerning priesthood, who shared their personal stories, their insights, and their advice in personal interviews, on the phone, and via e-mail. We are especially grateful to David Scoma, who coordinates the Vocation Discernment Board on America Online.

We extend a special thanks to the priests of the Diocese of Buffalo. We would like to acknowledge Father Richard Siepka, Rector, and Father Joseph Gatto, Vice Rector, of Christ the King Seminary, and the seminarians who took time from their busy schedule for a group interview. We are also grateful to Father Bonaventure Hayes, OFM, the legendary Library Director at Christ the King Seminary, who pointed us to the right section of the library on many occasions.

We would like to thank Monsignor Paul Burkard and Father Timothy Reker for helping us to understand the intricacies of the vocation process and priestly formation. Special thanks also go to Monsignor John Madsen, who kept us honest. We are also indebted to Father Patrick Lynch, SJ, and Father Benjamin Fiore, SJ, who kept us accurate in the best tradition of the Jesuits.

To Bishop Henry Mansell, we send our deepest gratitude for his support and encouragement. We owe Bishop Paul Loverde a special debt of thanks for his insights and advice, and for the Afterword he contributed to this book.

Lastly, we would like to thank all of you, who read this book as part of the discernment process. What is shared in this book is not just a collection of individual stories, but the universal journey we all share. Whether or not you become a priest doesn't matter. Thank you for taking the time and the energy to search for a deeper understanding of what God is asking of you.

COULD YOU EVER BECOME A CATHOLIC PRIEST?

CHAPTER 1

Could You Ever Become a Catholic Priest?

"I am 34 years old, and I am discerning the priesthood after 12 successful years in my career. I have many reasons not to consider becoming a priest. I always expected a wife and kids, and it is difficult to think I would exclude that option. I also have some trouble letting go of this 'investment' in my career. I never thought about the priesthood until age 32 or so, and it is all hitting me like a ton of bricks now. I think the decision would have been easier 10 years ago." Christopher Jeffrey, West Minneapolis, Minnesota

"I am 15. The first time I thought about the priesthood was when I made my First Communion. I thought about how great it would be to help people receive God. I'd get to know every person in that church. I'd help kids out during Reconciliation. During Mass, I'd explain the readings in my own words and how they relate to people's lives. But on the other side, I'd like to have a family. I'd want a son to play baseball with and a daughter to look after. God will have to help me make my decision." Michael Buscaglia, Amherst, New York

"I am 25 years old, in good health, with a good job, and yet I feel drawn to the priesthood. So my question is: has

1

anyone ever felt: *Hey, God, you can't mean me! I'm just a normal guy like all the others. Do you really want me to be a priest?"* Nicholas Zientarski, Smithtown, New York

Struggling with the idea of priesthood is very difficult today. The number of young priests and seminarians has declined drastically. Tough issues have arisen about celibacy, married priests, women priests, and gay priests. Questions loom as to the role of the laity versus the role of the priest. Society has become more secular and materialistic. Scandals in the Church have rocked the foundation of trust between people and priests. The unconditional respect and reverence that priests once held has been replaced with suspicion, and sometimes, scorn. Most parents don't encourage their sons to become priests. Most priests and religious don't encourage vocations either. Only 18% of young people recently surveyed by the Center for Applied Research in the Apostolate (CARA) in Washington, DC, said they had been encouraged by a priest, sister, or brother to consider a Church vocation.

"There's been a growing mistrust of religion in the world to the point where people relegate it into the realm of not important in their lives," suggests Monsignor Paul Burkard, former Vocation Director for the Diocese of Buffalo, who currently serves as pastor of a large suburban parish in Orchard Park, New York. "There's also the general dissolution of family life. People can't commit themselves to very much these days. In addition, young people today have more options than at any other time in human history. They come to maturity later in life so they make decisions about their adult life later. By the time they get to the maturity level where they might choose priesthood, they've already chosen marriage, a profession, or something else that would exclude priesthood."

Some say the problem of vocations would be solved if the Church ordained women. However, in May 1994, Pope John Paul II stated unequivocally that the Church has "no authority whatsoever to confer priestly ordination on women." He substantiates his point on the basis that Jesus chose only men as his apostles. Since

Jesus often moved against the cultural mores of the times, the fact that he did not choose women when he could have is an indication to the Pope that only men should be ordained to the priesthood.

In the wake of this statement, theologians debated the Pope's position. In November 1995, the Congregation for the Doctrine of the Faith reaffirmed the Pope's teaching and emphasized that there should be no further discussion on this point.

Some people say that allowing priests to marry would solve the vocation shortage. However, declining numbers of male seminarians in mainline Protestant denominations, which allow married clergy, seem to indicate that marital status is not the only factor in what some call a vocation crisis.

"There is certainly a decrease in the number of people becoming priests right now, but I think it's a crisis in awareness of what priesthood is all about," says Bishop Paul S. Loverde, Chairman of the National Conference of Catholic Bishops' Committee on Vocations. "It's a crisis in awareness of the wonder and awe of acting in this world in the person of Christ Jesus. I think that's where the crisis is."

In spite of these conflicting opinions, Catholic men in all age groups still admit that the thought of priesthood has crossed their mind at one time or another.

> "My first thought about the possibility of becoming a priest came when I was in fifth grade. As an altar boy, I would admire the priest as he prayed the Mass. His piety and lifestyle appealed to me." Michael Cuddy, Stamford, Connecticut

> "Through high school, I did not think about priesthood at all. I had struggles with my faith at that time as well. After my freshman year in college, God brought me back to a reconversion, and thoughts of the priesthood or religious life came with it. It was like: *Wow! This might really be where God is calling me!*" Phil Hurley, Baltimore, Maryland

"When I was in middle school, I was curious about the
priesthood. I requested a lot of information. Of course, I
was not mature enough to make a decision. But that was
my first 'call.' I graduated from high school and went to
college. I have been working as a counselor in a State program, although what I really like is to teach. Now, I am
29, and I still find a 'hole in my life.' I think the priesthood
will fill that gap." Javier Tirado, Miami, Florida

Maybe you've had thoughts about the priesthood off and on
over the years. Maybe you still feel the pull and keep trying to reject it. Maybe you've just begun to think about it. Chances are, if
you're struggling with the idea of priesthood, you probably feel
somewhat confused, frightened, and alone. You might not know
where to turn for accurate information or unbiased advice. Or you
might not be ready to take some action that would call attention
to whatever stirrings you feel inside you.

"Most of our friends and family have a hard time understanding what it means to be called. It took me years to
realize that there were other people of all ages who had
gone through or were just starting to go through the heavy
questioning that I found myself facing. I wish I had found
more people like that earlier in my own discernment."
David Scoma, Maitland, Florida

The purpose of this book is not to persuade or coerce you into
pursuing a vocation to the priesthood. No one can do that anyway.
The decision as to what you will do with your life is always a free
choice, which no one — not even God — will force you to make.

The purpose of this book is to allow you to explore in a safe
and private way some of the issues, questions and concerns revolv-
ing around a vocation to the priesthood. In the following chapters,
you will meet priests, seminarians, and men currently considering
the priesthood. They will share their stories and offer insights and
advice. In the process, you may discover that God is calling you to

the priesthood. Or you may discover that God is calling you to spend your life in some other way. The first step, however, is to explore the question: What is a vocation?

Chapter Notes

Most parents don't encourage their sons... and f.: CARA *Compendium of Vocations Research*, Bryan T. Froehle, PhD, editor, Washington, DC, Center for Applied Research in the Apostolate, 1997.

Pope John Paul II stated unequivocally...: Pope John Paul II, *Ordinatio sacerdotalis*, May, 1994.

However, declining numbers of male seminarians...: CARA *Compendium of Vocations Research*, p. ix.

CHAPTER 2

What is a Vocation?

"I am a freshman in high school, and I think I may be a priest when I get older." Brett McLaughlin, Pittsford, New York

"I know I have some calling, but I want to know if anyone has good experience in helping to discern these areas?" Brandon Darling, Illinois

"My own experience has convinced me that a calling to religious life or the priesthood is a pure gift. There's no other way to explain it!" Father Marvin Kitten, SJ, New Orleans, Louisiana

If you're looking for a simple definition of a vocation, the literal meaning of the word is a "call." But a vocation is more than an ordinary call. A vocation is a call from God, and anyone who has felt God's call knows that the process is anything but simple.

While most people think of a vocation as what they are called to *do* in life, it's important to understand that the first and most important call from God is the universal call to holiness.

Syndicated columnist Father John Catoir came to this understanding during his college days. He felt stirrings in his heart about the priesthood, but he also felt drawn to the married life. His spiri-

7

tual director, Father James McCoy, SJ, warned him not to confuse a call to holiness with a call to a specific vocation, such as marriage, the single life, or the priesthood. "The call to holiness is universal," Father McCoy insisted. "All Christians are called to it. At present you are wrestling with a call to holiness; that is certain. But that does not necessarily mean that you should be a priest. You've got to get that straight!"

This distinction between a call to holiness and a call to a specific vocation is important. Some of the greatest saints were called to holiness, but not to the priesthood. Likewise, some of the greatest scandals in the Church were caused by men who came into the priesthood for reasons other than holiness.

The universal call to holiness is rooted in our baptism. It is a call to know, love and serve the Lord. It is a movement within the soul that draws us toward a deeper union with God. We feel a growing desire to love God and to love our neighbor. We come to understand that there is a reason for our existence, and there is meaning in our lives. We begin to catch a glimpse of who we are in relation to God.

For Father Joseph Rogliano this moment of truth came during his second year in the seminary when his spiritual director asked the simple question: "Who are you?"

"He didn't care about my name, my address, my family members," Father Rogliano recalls. "He kept probing. He was trying to lead me to acknowledge my identity as a child of God who was seeking to discern what to do with the gift of my life. The breaking point came when I professed for the first time that I was connected to Jesus. I identified the Lord as the giver of gifts. I acknowledged that I was trying to respond to Him and to use the gift of life that He gave me as best I could. As soon as I said that, I started crying. It was a crucial time for me. It was a real turning point."

The universal call to holiness is an ongoing conversion experience. It keeps opening our eyes to new awareness of God's loving presence. It keeps inviting us to turn toward God by aligning our will with God's will.

"God moves us to move ourselves freely," explain Marie

Theresa Coombs and Francis Kelly Nemeck, OMI, in *Called by God: A Theology of Vocations and Lifelong Commitment*:

> God's willing moves our will to freely desire what God wills for us. Because we are free, a wide range of responses are possible. Sometimes we experience our freedom with spontaneity and joy. At other times we find our freedom perplexing and painful. Yet the Lord works with each response, drawing us, transforming us. When we say "yes," the Lord incites us to deeper commitment. When we insist on "no," God works toward conversion. When we persist with "maybe," the Lord prods us out of indecision.

Father Emile Briere, an 80-year-old Madonna House priest who lives in a one-room cabin in the Canadian woods, has seen this internal drama played out in men and women who come from all over the world to seek his advice on what direction their lives should take. "If they come and say, 'I'd like to know what my vocation is,' I tell them there are two steps. The first step is: 'Do you want to do God's will?' If a person says, 'I'm not sure I want to do God's will,' I tell them to go pray about that. When they can say yes to the first question, they can come back and we'll talk about number two."

Father John Powell, SJ, believes that a willingness to do God's will is built on two convictions: "I have to believe that God loves me more than I love myself and that he wants my happiness more than I want it," he explains. "And I have to believe that God knows more than I do about what will make me truly happy. I have a feeling that if God had given me everything I ever asked for, I would now be seriously unhappy. I think that one basis of my desire to find and do God's will should be this: His will is my only chance to be truly and lastingly happy."

Father Michael Scanlon, TOR, President of Franciscan University of Steubenville, came to this junction when he was returning from Mass one morning in March 1954. He literally stopped in his tracks when he heard an inner voice saying, "Will you give your life to me?"

I knew God was speaking to me. I had never heard God
speak to me that way before, but I knew it was Him.
I didn't answer immediately. I knew why. I was asking myself, "If I say 'Yes' what will He do with my life?" I didn't
want to answer this way because I did not want to refuse
God or be ungrateful to Him. I also thought this is a moment of grace; I didn't want to lose an opportunity that
might pass and not return.
Finally, I struggled out a "Yes." But I cautiously added, "Can
I wait to give you my life until I finish law school and pass
the bar?" That seemed to be acceptable to God.

Father Scanlon discovered that after surrendering his life to
God, he felt a constant pull to seek and understand God's will. He
began to recognize the need to make God the center of his life.

"The object of every vocation is God," he explains. "It's not
building a better society, renewing the Church, having a family,
fulfilling yourself, helping people, or confronting new challenges.
All these things may be involved in a vocation, but the primary
objective — the goal of the priest or sister, husband or wife, single
lay man or lay woman — is to love God."

While God calls all of us to lives of holiness, we see in Scripture, in the history of the Church, in the stories of the saints, and
in the lives of people around us that the Lord also selects certain
individuals for special missions or ministries. "God has created me
to do Him some definite service," wrote Cardinal John Henry
Newman. "He has committed some work to me which He has not
committed to another."

A vocation to the priesthood is a very specific call from God.
In 1993, the National Conference of Catholic Bishops reaffirmed
that while all of the baptized participate in the priesthood of Christ,
"priests are especially configured to Christ to act in His person as
head and pastor of the Church and in the name of the whole people
of God. Priests are ministers who receive their sacred authority from
Christ through the Church."

"The Scripture is very clear: 'You have not chosen Me. I have chosen you' (Jn 15:16). It makes a big difference. If the approach to a religious vocation is you making the choice, you can put it in the same category as choosing to become a doctor or lawyer. A vocation to the priesthood really doesn't belong in that category. It is God calling you to this." Father Bob Fagan, Allentown, Pennsylvania

Sometimes, people seem to know without a doubt that God is calling them to the priesthood:

"Why do I feel called? It seems like every aspect of my life has led me to this destination. I remember being in middle school and feeling called. I am constantly amazed by people. I am grieved by the injustices in the world. I want to help people grow in their relationship with God and with other people. I am not interested in material gain. I've had several opportunities at marriage but nothing ever seemed to work out. A calling to the priesthood is something I've felt for a long time." Charles Burt, Austin, Texas

Other people discover that they are not called to the priesthood:

"Plenty of people feel called, but for different reasons. Out of all those people, God does not choose for each of them to actually enter religious life. For some of us, there is a lesson to be learned in the call itself — whether it is a call to bring us close to the Lord, to lead us on a different path in life, or simply to teach us lessons about ourselves, others, and God that we couldn't learn any other way." David Scoma, Maitland, Florida

Sometimes the call is not recognized:

"I found that I wasn't listening to God. I was listening to the TV and radio. My priorities weren't straight. They were all crooked. Not that I was a bad guy. When I invited God back into my life, I realized that he had never stopped talking. He was talking when I wasn't listening! I think a lot of guys need to LISTEN." Nicholas Zientarski, Smithtown, New York

In most cases, people struggle with some degree of uncertainty. They want to do God's will, and they may feel an attraction to the priesthood, but the call is not clear enough to make a commitment. They begin a process called discernment.

"I am a firm believer in the fact that God will never give any of us a challenge without also providing the grace to deal with it. Discernment is exactly that — trying to determine God's will for each of us." BKL, Birmingham, Alabama

There is no standard formula for the way in which God calls people to the priesthood. There is no explanation why some people seem to know instantly, while others agonize for months or years. Pope John Paul II points out that every vocation to the priesthood has "an individual history of its own, related to quite specific moments in the life of each one of us." In the next chapter, we'll take a closer look at some of the different ways in which God has called people to the priesthood.

Chapter Notes

"God moves us to move ourselves freely...": Marie Theresa Coombs and Francis Kelly Nemeck, OMI, *Called By God: A Theology of Vocations and Lifelong Commitment*, Collegeville, Minnesota: The Liturgical Press, 1992, p. 16.

"I have to believe that God loves me more...": John Powell, SJ, *Through the Eyes of Faith*, Allen, Texas: Tabor Publishing, 1992, pp. 24-25.

"Will you give your life to me?": Michael Scanlon, TOR, *What Does God Want?*, Huntington, Indiana: Our Sunday Visitor Publishing Division, 1996, p. 7.

"The object of every vocation is God...": *Ibid.*, p. 90.

"God has created me to do Him some definite service...": John Henry Newman, *Meditations and Devotions*, 400-1.

"priests are especially configured...": *Program of Priestly Formation*, Fourth Edition, [30] National Conference of Catholic Bishops, 1993, p. 8.

"an individual history of its own...": Pope John Paul II, "Letter to Priests for Holy Thursday 1996," *L'Osservatore Romano*, March 27, 1996.

CHAPTER 3

How God Calls †

"I really believe that my call to the priesthood came when I was a senior in high school. In church one day, something inside me said, 'You should be a priest.'" Father James Ciupek, Williamsville, New York

"It wasn't just one moment when I felt a tap on the shoulder and a voice said, 'This is right.' It was more ongoing affirmation along the way." Father Richard Siepka, East Aurora, New York

"I think vocations come in a lot of different ways. Some people get zapped and all of a sudden they know. Then there are those of us who just plod along." Monsignor John Madsen, Depew, New York

Father Brian McSweeney first thought about the priesthood in third grade. "From that point on it was all I wanted to be — that is, until high school hit," he recalls. Teachers, guidance counselors, friends, and family members began to pressure him to do well in school so he could get into a good college and be successful. He followed their advice. After high school, he enrolled at Georgetown University. Once again, people advised him to do well in school so he could get a good job and be successful.

"I think in the back of my mind was always the thought of a vocation," he admits, "but it was pushed far back."

After graduating from Georgetown with a degree in business, he worked his way up the ladder in several New York City banks. During his spare time, he earned a Masters Degree in Business Administration, which offered the promise of making him even more successful.

"I bought a condo in Scarsdale," he recalls. "I vacationed in the Hamptons. I achieved all that society said was 'successful,' but I knew I was not complete. In my heart I knew something was missing. I searched for it in my childhood yearning to be a priest, and I found it. My first night in the pre-seminary program, I knew the peace of doing God's will."

Father McSweeney's story is somewhat typical of the way in which young men enter the priesthood today. The average age of today's seminarian is 29 as opposed to the typical 25-year-old seminarian in 1966. In fact, 28 percent of today's seminarians are 25-29; 21 percent are 30-34; 11 percent are 35-39; and 13 percent are over 40. About half of today's seminarians have some business or professional experience. They all acknowledge some sense that God is calling them to the priesthood. But the ways they experience the call contain some striking similarities as well as some distinct differences.

For many, the call to priesthood begins with an intuition or a feeling. "Usually the first perceptions of a calling to a basic vocational lifestyle consist in a nebulous leaning in a certain direction," explain Marie Theresa Coombs and Francis Kelly Nemeck, OMI. "At the outset, this vague attraction is without specific form or forethought. We feel an inclination, but without especially adverting to it. The inclination is untested and not necessarily viewed in terms of choice or commitment. Our vocation at this state is still fundamentally preconscious and pre-reflective."

For some, this first inclination toward priesthood happens during childhood:

"I was in second grade. I hadn't even made my First Communion yet, when a priest asked me to be an altar server. It was Mother's Day. My older brother was serving, and the priest put a cassock on me and said, 'You're going to serve Mass.' That's when my thoughts of the priesthood first started." Father David LiPuma, Buffalo, New York

For others, it happens in early adolescence:

"I first thought about becoming a priest when I was in seventh or eighth grade. It was triggered by a vocations talk from the Salesians." Father Gary Bagley, Williamsville, New York

Sometimes, the initial call to the priesthood comes during the later teenage years:

"The summer between my sophomore and junior year in high school, I was sick with poison ivy and I couldn't move. I started reading Maryknoll Magazines and my heart was touched by the pictures and the quotations from St. Paul." Father Vincent O'Malley, CM, Niagara Falls, New York

In other cases, it happens in college:

"When I was a freshman in college, my pastor asked if I had ever thought about the priesthood. He shared the story of his life with me. This impressed me a lot because he was a very private person. He invited me to go on a retreat. It started me thinking." Father Leon Biernat, Tonawanda, New York

Sometimes, the idea emerges after college when a young man begins to consider possible career paths:

"I had graduated from college and had done a tour of duty with the Marines. After my discharge from the military, I went to a job fair. A vocation director for the Vincentians shoved some information into my backpack and said, 'Don't let your girlfriend see this!'" Father Kevin Creagh, CM, Niagara Falls, New York

Other times, the first stirrings do not occur until after someone has already set out on a different career path:

"I was working as a psychiatric nurse in New Haven and I was interested in pursuing a Masters Degree in pastoral counseling or in psychiatric nursing. I went to Boston College to inquire about their programs. As I was walking across the campus on that beautiful sunny day, the thought came to me out of nowhere: 'You are going to become a priest.' I remember that thought filling me with tremendous joy. Then I thought, 'How can this be?' But I chose to pursue it." Father Don Guglielmi, East Haven, Connecticut

The way in which God calls a person is always personal and unique. Some priests and seminarians will tell you they had mystical experiences and heard the voice of God or felt the presence of Jesus. Some say Our Lady was instrumental in their call:

"I had just finished my third year of university in Toronto, and maybe I was praying a little more intensely than I had been before, but I began to experience Our Lady's presence for the first time. It wasn't just one experience. It was two or three different experiences — one in a local parish and a couple of times in my prayer. I didn't have any devotion to Mary growing up as a child, but suddenly I began to experience her presence. After that, within three months, I felt this strong call to the priesthood coming to the surface. The Scripture passage, 'The harvest is great but the laborers are few' (Mt 9:37), became very strong in my spirit and I wanted to respond to that. It was a real gift. I believe that the Lord gave me his mother and gave me the call through her." Father Roger Vandenakker, Ottawa, Ontario

Some priests say they experienced nothing more than a fleeting thought about the priesthood during prayer. Others describe an intense internal struggle:

"In sixth grade a nun suggested that we say three Hail Mary's a day so we would know what our vocation in life might be. In March of my junior year in high school, I was praying those Hail Mary's and the thought of religious life struck me. My immediate reaction was fear. I didn't know what a priest should be. I couldn't imagine myself as a priest. I tried to picture myself in a cassock with my hands folded. It just wasn't me. For the next two weeks, I really wrestled with this like Jacob wrestled with God (Gn 32:23-32). I tried to come up with every reason why I could not, should not, would not become a priest. At the end of that period, I was drained. I could not come up with any reason that would satisfy me as to why I should not become a priest. Then, and only then, did I begin to think positively of the priesthood." Father Bob Fagan, Allentown, Pennsylvania

Many priests look back over their early lives and see that God called them in very ordinary ways:

"I can't come up with one specific moment when I thought about it for the first time. I grew up in a Catholic culture in which priests were always around so it was a natural thing. I lived next to a rectory. Priests were my neighbors. My distant cousin was a diocesan priest. I grew up with the possibility that I could do that, too." Father Richard Siepka, East Aurora, New York

Sometimes, admiration toward someone in religious life evolved into the idea of following in those footsteps:

"I can pinpoint the very day when I first began to think seriously about entering the Jesuits. I was 16, and I had been invited by a Jesuit scholastic, who was one of my teachers, to go to New York and watch a television broadcast. He told me to meet him at St. Peter's. When I got there, a couple of scholastics came down the stairs and I saw them as human beings who seemed very happy to be together. It was that which began my thinking." Father James Hennesey, SJ, LeMoyne College, Syracuse, New York

While good role models are often a factor, God can also use bad experiences as a way of drawing someone to the priesthood:

"I wanted to be a priest from both positive and negative experiences. When I was in grade school my grandparents were having quite a bit of difficulty with their marriage. The parish priest would come to the house to talk to them. He helped them to continue toward a good marriage. It was this same priest who would take the altar servers across the street for ice cream after the novena on Tuesday night. I had a positive image of the priesthood from him. The negative came from a priest whose preaching was constantly telling people how bad they were. I also had a few bad experiences with a priest in the confessional as a teenager. I remember wanting to replace these guys so no one else would ever get a bad deal. I look back at all that and see that God used those experiences. For me, that's where the grace of God was." Monsignor John Madsen, Depew, New York

God frequently uses other people as instruments in the vocation process. In fact, some vocation directors believe a personal invitation is a key component in helping a person to recognize God's call. Prior to the Second Vatican Council (1962-1965), sisters in Catholic school rooms would ask if thoughts of the priesthood had ever crossed anyone's mind. "Some of them would take you by the ear, lead you to Father, and say, 'This boy should go to the seminary!'," quips Father Paul Golden, CM, President of Niagara University in Lewiston, New York.

"I was an altar boy. I sang in the choir. I answered phones in the rectory. But it wasn't until some sisters asked me if I ever considered being a priest that I actually thought of it. I was around priests a lot, but it never occurred to me to think of myself doing what they did. I had to be asked." Father Chris Heath, Tustin, California

Increasingly, lay people have started to recognize possible candidates for priesthood:

"When I was a senior at the University of Kentucky, the Diocese of Lexington ran a 'Called By Name' program where people were asked to send in the name of someone they thought would make a good priest. A few days later, a priest from the Newman Center called me and said, 'Jim, your name was submitted seven times by seven different people. Have you ever thought about the priesthood?' My first reaction was, 'Oh, come on!' But it got me thinking. I started to wonder if maybe I could be a priest." Father Jim Bastian, Amherst, New York

Sometimes, the prodding comes from a friend:

"When I decided to switch careers, I started looking into teaching. My best friend, who is an atheist on a bad day and an agnostic on a good day, said, 'What about your faith? Whenever you come over for dinner you always want to pray. You always want to stop by a church. You don't just go to church on Sundays, you go two, three, four days during the week. Obviously this stuff is not a burden to you. Why don't you consider the priesthood?' He got me thinking, and I started to pray about it." Father Ted Jost, Tonawanda, New York

Sometimes, the prodding comes from a complete stranger:

"When I was in sixth grade, I wrestled with the idea of priesthood. I told God that He was crazy, and I wanted nothing to do with it. I decided to go to a public high school and a State college so I wouldn't be forced into anything. While I was in college, I went to the placement office one day to check out career possibilities. The placement officer asked me what I wanted to do. I told her about my grandmother and how she was dying of cancer. I told her I wanted to help alleviate some of the pain and suffering in the world. I was actually thinking about the possibility of a career in biology, but she tossed a vocation booklet into my lap and said, 'Have you ever looked at one of these?' I felt like I had gotten clubbed down by a person that I never met before. Here was a perfect stranger in a secular school who asked me if I wanted to be a priest!" Father Robert Wozniak, Buffalo, New York

If there is a common denominator in all of these stories, it's that God reaches out to people in ways that are individual and highly personal. It's not unusual, however, for people to feel somewhat confused and uncertain. "People come and say, 'I think I feel called to the priesthood, but I don't know what that means,'" explains Monsignor Paul Burkard. "So they begin to ask questions that will clarify the call and help them to understand whether they are competent to do this."

Chapter Notes

The average age of today's seminarian... and f.: CARA Compendium of Vocations Research, 1997, p. 7.

About half of today's seminarians... and f.: Eugene F. Hemrick and James J. Walsh, Seminarians in the Nineties. A National Study of Seminarians in Theology, National Catholic Educational Association, 1993.

"Usually the first perceptions of a calling...": Called by God, p. 86-87.

CHAPTER 4

I Feel Called to the Priesthood, but...

"It happened during adoration at World Youth Day in Denver. I had been watching the Franciscan friars all week, and during adoration, this thought came into my mind very clearly: 'That is what I want to be.' Then, I thought: 'What does that mean? Is God calling me to be a priest or a brother or something? Is this possible?' I knew that I needed to talk to someone about this!" Phil Hurley, Baltimore, Maryland

"After the priest at the Newman Center asked if I had ever thought about becoming a priest, I started to wonder if I could be. If I had not known any priests, I would have just laughed it off. Having known Father Dan, it was a legitimate thing to consider. I started to think, 'Can I see myself in that capacity?'" Father Jim Bastian, Amherst, New York

"While attending a youth retreat, I was struck by a talk given by a priest about his own vocation. A strong question came to me which basically asked: 'Is there any reason you are not doing that?' The question was insistent and I didn't have a good answer. Thus began not a certainty about my calling, but a certainty of the need for serious discernment about God's will for my life." Mark Mossa, Grand Coteau, Louisiana

After he passed the bar exam, Father Michael Scanlon, TOR, realized that God was calling him to the priesthood, but he wasn't sure what that meant. He had stopped going to Catholic school after eighth grade. He didn't know much about Catholicism. When he thought of religious orders, he thought Jesuit, so he went to see the Jesuits.

"The vocation is the restless spirit of God within you," Father Avery Dulles, SJ, told him. "You keep following it to the place it's at rest and poured out."

Marie Theresa Coombs and Francis Kelly Nemeck, OMI, describe this restless spirit as "a torrent welling up from within us but not of us." A vocation is not something that we initiate or direct. It is something that unfolds, and we are free to accept the invitation or refuse. "The Lord does not force or coerce us," they note, "yet God most surely pursues and, if need be, overpowers us (Jr 20:7-9). The Lord does not manipulate or trick us, but neither will God let us get away indefinitely with resistance (Gn 32:23-32). The Lord persists in working with our freedom until we are free enough to choose rightly."

> "I had the calling to the priesthood a long time ago. I was young and I wanted to ignore it. I am now a nurse, but I am not happy doing this, and I wonder if it is because of ignoring the call." T.R.N., Watertown, Massachusetts

It's not a sin to refuse a vocation. God will not punish you for saying no. "Vocation is free," explains Father Raymond Hostie, SJ. "This is why certain moralists say that failure to heed a vocation does not constitute a sin. It should be stressed, however, that such a refusal does at least constitute the missing of an important opportunity."

When Father James Keller, founder of The Christophers, decided to leave the seminary to work in the family business, nagging doubts plagued him. "I've about decided not to go back," he told a neighborhood priest.

And then, in the hope that he would back me up, I asked
him if he didn't agree that my decision was wise.
To my surprise, he emphatically replied: "No, I'm not going to take it on my conscience to tell you not to go back
to the seminary! After all, in God's plan, there may be thousands of people whose salvation depends on what you may
do for them as a priest." He may have said more, but that
statement was enough.
I began to see that failure on my part to be an instrument
of the divine plan could, in a minor way at least, deprive
others of blessings that rightfully belonged to them and
that were to be sent through one person like myself.

Monsignor Paul Burkard advises men, who feel that God might
be calling, to enter some kind of a discernment process and find
out what all of this really means. "That's a big step for people," he
admits. "But if they don't do it now, they're going to come back at
age 30 or 40 or 50 and say, 'I've been thinking about this all my
life, and it's still there, and I don't know what to do.' My sense is
that if you have the feeling that somehow the priesthood is attractive to you, take the time to look into it."

"I took a year off after college to think about it. I worked
at K-mart." Father Robert Wozniak, Buffalo, New York

Making a commitment to set aside time for discernment is a
good thing. You don't have to commit yourself to an entire year.
But it is a good idea to commit yourself to a daily, weekly, or
monthly time schedule when you can work on discernment.
One of the things Father M. Basil Pennington, OCSO, suggests as part of the discernment process is to establish what he calls
"a rule of life." Simply stated, a rule of life is a daily, weekly, and
monthly schedule in which you set aside specific times for prayer,
study, work, meals, exercise, recreation, reading, and other priorities.
"Some people react to the idea of a rule; 'rule' for them con-

notes something binding, a cage which will inhibit growth," he explains. "It should rather be taken as something supporting life, a trellis which allows the climber to reach up toward the sun of justice. Much of the time a vital plant reaches out on its own, away from the trellis. But when it needs help to keep growing in the upward direction it wants to pursue, it has the trellis to lean on for support."

A rule of life is a discipline that you impose upon yourself. While it does "bind" you to specific activities each day, it also frees you from unwanted or unnecessary distractions. When you live according to a rule of life, you have better balance and control over your activities.

"Life is monotonous if it has no goal or purpose," wrote Bishop Fulton J. Sheen. "When we do not know why we are here or where we are going, then life is full of frustrations and unhappiness; when there is no goal or overall purpose, people generally concentrate on motion. Instead of working toward an ideal, they keep changing the ideal and calling it 'progress.' They do not know where they are going, but they are certainly 'on their way.'"

A rule of life gives you the perfect excuse when someone or something intrudes on your prayer time or some other priority: *"I already have something scheduled right now, but I do have some free time this afternoon."*

In developing your rule of life, Father Pennington suggests that you take four sheets of paper. On the first sheet, write down what you want out of life. On the second sheet, list what you need to do in order to obtain what you want, such as food, sleep, study, friendship, exercise, prayer, etc. On the third sheet, reflect on the last six months and list the things that have prevented you from doing what is really important in your life. On the fourth sheet, begin to formulate your rule of life on a daily, weekly, or monthly basis. Some people create a daily schedule with times for getting up, prayer, exercise, a shower, breakfast, etc. There may also be special things that you want to block in weekly or monthly, such as a weekly fast day or a monthly day of reflection.

"Often the rule of life will need revision to respond to the onward flow of life," Father Pennington explains. "There is joy in realizing that our lives are moving in the direction we want instead of getting pushed around by circumstances and events."

What are some other elements that could be incorporated into your life?

Sister Kathleen Bryant, RSC, a Vocation Director for the Archdiocese of Los Angeles, offers eight suggestions for those who are in the early stages of thinking about the priesthood or religious life.

• Pray: "Expose yourself in a conscious way to God's presence. God is bombarding us with His blessings and presence everywhere and at all times but we are often closed."

• Get a Notebook: "Start writing down what you experience.... Are there any particular events that started you thinking about a vocation to the priesthood or religious life? Any Scripture texts that struck you to the core?"

• Remember: "Recall your personal faith history. Where have you been? When did you first experience God? How has your image of God changed since you were a child?"

• Talk to Someone You Can Trust: "Talk to one person. In the early stages of discernment, don't tell your family and friends. They may start treating you differently and not give you the freedom to genuinely discern your call."

• Start Looking Around: "Gently start looking around at the priests and religious you have known. Pick up your local Catholic newspaper, magazine, or directory to notice ads for vocation events, retreats, and other activities."

• Get Involved: "Get involved in some form of service or parish ministry (teaching religious education class, serving as lector, minister of the Eucharist, visiting the elderly, feeding the homeless)."

• Enlist the Support of Prayerful People: "Ask people to pray for you. You don't have to specify an intention."

• Pay Attention: "Notice and pay attention to what is life-giving, energizing for you. What sparks fly out at you in your life? Where's the passion? the attraction? Write any incidents, relationships, Scriptures, etc., in your notebook. They are all pointers and clues."

Out of all these suggestions, prayer is the most important. An hour in prayer every day is the ideal for someone who is discerning a vocation to the priesthood. If you're just beginning the process, however, an hour may be too much. Starting with ten or twenty minutes everyday is probably more realistic.

"A priest told me that I should spend at least twenty minutes in prayer a day. Well, I sat down the first time and suddenly I was not sure what I was supposed to do. I began to wonder what is prayer anyway?" D.J.C., New York

Since ancient times, the simplest definition of prayer is "keeping company with God." Father Mark Illig, Director of the Pope John Paul II Residence, a house of discernment for men considering the priesthood in the Diocese of Buffalo, suggests three ways to begin forming a strong relationship with the Lord:

• Pray with the Scriptures. Take a short passage from Scripture, read it slowly, and let the message sink into your heart. St. Ignatius Loyola suggests that you use your imagination to place yourself in the Bible passage. Imagine the smells, the sights, the sounds. What is Jesus saying to you in this passage? What is your reaction to this message?

• Take time for devotional prayer. The rosary and devotions to the saints are all very basic, but they help us to form good habits of prayer. These kinds of prayers are often simple enough that they can be prayed while you're waiting in line, when you're riding the bus, or at odd moments. No one will even know that you're doing it.

• Experiment with meditation or contemplative prayer. This

kind of prayer involves quieting yourself down for a period of time so that God can speak to you. Begin by slowly reciting the name of Jesus over and over again for twenty minutes. You will start to feel yourself calming down and a quiet sense of God's presence will envelop you.

Father Illig tells men in the discernment process to pay attention to the feelings that they are having during prayer. "A lot of people say that your feelings are not really important because feelings come and go," he says. "I think that feelings during prayer offer you some valuable clues. If you present something to the Lord and you feel a deep abiding peace, it is usually a sign the Lord is leading you in the right direction."

> "I went to Medjugorje on pilgrimage. Every day in prayer I would ask, 'God, do you want me to be a priest?' Every time I asked, a clear, strong 'Yes!' welled up in my heart. Sometimes I heard, 'Yes, I've been trying to tell you that for a while.' This continued for all nine days that I was there. I became very much at peace, and I was pretty much convinced that this was God's call." Terry Donahue, Ottawa, Ontario

In addition to personal prayer, daily participation in the Eucharist is essential. Before going to sleep, a daily examination of conscience is also important. This involves a review of good and bad experiences during the day, accepting responsibility for your actions, and surrendering yourself to God's love and mercy.

You might want to acquaint yourself with the *Liturgy of the Hours*, sometimes called the breviary, which is a collection of psalms, readings, and prayers that are chanted seven times a day in monasteries. The American bishops call it "the song of praise, which shapes a life of prayer around the mysteries of the Lord celebrated in the liturgical year. The liturgy of the Church becomes the leaven of priestly prayer and a hallmark of all forms of spirituality."

Prayer will open you to an exciting, new awareness of God

and an increased understanding of your own spiritual dimension. As you move more deeply into your prayer life, new questions will arise along with new opportunities to find the answers.

> "I always pictured myself as having a wife, two kids, and the house with the picket fence. How do priests give that up?" John Betts, Alexandria, Virginia

"I'm working with a guy right now who is caught in this situation," admits Monsignor Paul Burkard. "He's in love and nearing engagement to a young lady. I think he's authentically in love with her, but he feels a real call to priesthood. He's on the fence."

Sister Kathleen Bryant recommends the model of discernment developed by St. Ignatius of Loyola. "St. Ignatius wrote the *Spiritual Exercises* out of his own experience of discerning the spirits," she explains. "As he lay in bed for several months recovering from a leg injury, he spent time reading and thinking. He read the lives of the saints and imagined himself doing great things for God as St. Francis and St. Dominic did. Being a soldier, he also imagined himself being victorious in battle, receiving honor and wooing and courting beautiful women. Ignatius noticed that both of these fantasies gave him joy and delight. Upon reflection though, he noticed that the joy evoked from being a great warrior and lover was not lasting. The fantasies about doing great things for God gave him a joy or consolation that was sustained over time. He noticed a difference in the quality of the joy."

> "The Ignatian method of 'discernment of spirits' proved helpful for me in coming to a final decision." Mark Mossa, Grand Coteau, Louisiana

The Ignatian method is not the only method of discernment, however. Father Michael Scanlon, TOR, suggests five tests to apply when making a major life decision: "Judge (1) its conformity to God's revealed will, (2) its contribution to the ongoing conversion of your heart, (3) its consistency with the way God has led you in the past, (4) how or whether it is confirmed, and (5) the degree of conviction in your heart about the rightness of the decision."

Many dioceses and religious orders offer discernment retreats at regular intervals for people who are considering the priesthood or religious life. During these sessions, the importance of prayer and reflection in the discernment process will be emphasized again. Father Scanlon suggests that people pose two questions in prayer: *Lord, is it your will that I do this?* and *Lord, is it your will that I not do this?*

"By comparing the internal responses to these two questions, the person often finds the answer," he notes. "Gentle questioning like this can give focus to one's prayer. We often talk too much in prayer and don't listen enough. But when we try to listen, we can be plagued by distractions and unfocused silence. Putting a question to the Lord can break us through the fog of paralysis and uncertainty and allow our heart to open to the will of God."

> "I kept asking God what He wanted me to do. He kept telling me over and over again to trust Him. After much prayer, I still had no idea what God wanted. 'Trust Me,' He kept saying. Finally, out of exasperation, I said, 'Okay. You want trust? I'll give you trust. I can't tell if You want me to be a priest or not, but I'm willing to take the chance that You do. If You want me to, then You better clear every obstacle and give me peace every step of the way. If You don't, then You better block any efforts.' I was really putting things on the line with God. As soon as I made this declaration, I felt so much relief. The decision was no longer on my shoulders. I gave it to God to work out." John Fletcher, Ottawa, Ontario

Reading is another important element in the discernment process. In a recent survey of seminarians, the list of authors that had the greatest influence on their decision to become priests included: Thomas Merton, Henri Nouwen, C.S. Lewis, St. Augustine, and St. Thomas Aquinas. Reading spiritual classics can also help you grow closer to God. "Whether it was the *Imitation of Christ*, the *Spiri-*

tual Exercises of St. Ignatius, the *Soul of the Apostolate,* or the *Introduction to a Devout Life,* the message was the same: There is a primitive face that you show only to God," explains Father David Chandler of Southwest Harbor, Maine.

As part of their reading, some men begin to collect books, magazines and vocation information about the diocesan priesthood or religious orders:

> "I have been receiving some information about the different orders, but I am still undecided. I pray every day to see if God can guide me through this process." Javier Tirado, Miami, Florida

Asking questions and soliciting the advice of other people is another important part of the process. "You need clear, straight talk on the meaning of priesthood," says Bishop Paul Loverde. "What does it mean to be acting in the person of Christ Jesus in the lives of human beings the way a priest can? Everyone has to represent the Lord in some way, but priests do that uniquely. We need straight talk about the necessity of priesthood. There would be no Church without the Eucharist, and there would be no Eucharist without ordained priests. Priests are a necessity. I don't know if people understand that."

> "I have been talking to many different people about this. I think it's smart to get all the different input that you can. But the one thing I have found is that unless the people you talk to have been praying about this, they are going to give you a worldly answer. The world is not going to tell you to become a priest. So take everyone's advice for what it's worth, and remember that this is really between you and God." Jason Vidmar, Davenport, Iowa

In order to make sure that the advice is spiritual and not worldly, Father Joseph Gatto, Vice Rector at Christ the King Seminary, encourages men considering the priesthood to find a spiritual director. "Find a priest whom you perceive to be a role model," he suggests. "You've got to be mentored through this. You need that kind of support. You need a spiritual director."

A good director will guide you in your prayer life and listen to the Holy Spirit speaking in your heart. The relationship between a director and a directee is always confidential so you can feel free to be open and honest. You will be asked to share your life history as well as your faith journey. You can ask questions and express your concerns openly. You can take a serious look at your strengths and weaknesses. You can examine your options.

> "I went through some of those dark nights when you start to question everything. I questioned my abilities, my calling, my relationship with God. I was trying to understand myself and what I really wanted from life. My spiritual director took me through that and helped me to discern." Father David LiPuma, Buffalo, New York

Volunteering in various ministries is also essential to the discernment process.

> "I volunteered with a group of Mother Teresa's brothers in Los Angeles, as well as teaching religious education classes and doing some other things around the parish." Father Ron Pecci, OFM, Holy Name Province

In a recent study, large numbers of seminarians reported that they had been active in their parishes as altar servers, lectors and Eucharistic ministers. "Second to service of the altar was involvement in religious education," the study noted. "This too should not be a surprise. Passing on the faith, teaching the truths of the faith, religious educators perform an essential task. This activity apparently led many of today's seminarians to seek to share in the role of official teachers of the faith as priests."

> "One technique I share with others in discernment is to imagine yourself doing what a priest does. When I was in

high school and was asked to consider a vocation, I would imagine myself doing what I knew priests did: saying Mass, hearing confessions, counseling, helping people in grief, preaching and teaching. I imagined myself doing these things and liked the image. This was enough for me to at least give the seminary a chance. I would occasionally re-visit these images as I went through the seminary, sort of as a measure of my continued interest. I suppose if I had ever lost my attraction to the idea of this life work, I would have considered it a sign not to be ordained." Father Chris Heath, Tustin, California

Other techniques include making a list of all the positive and negative aspects of the priesthood, or making a list of your gifts and talents and comparing them to the qualities needed in a priest. You might want to write a letter to God and then imagine how God would respond to you. St. Ignatius suggests that you imagine your-self on your death bed and think about what would have been the best way to spend your life.

Don't be surprised if throughout the discernment process, the question that lurks in your mind is: *How do I know that what I feel inside of me is authentically from God?*

"There's a search for some security," explains Monsignor Burkard. "People want to know if the priesthood is really what God is calling them to do."

You may wish that God would just appear to you in a flash or speak to you in a dream so you would know for sure. There have been rare occasions when God has called people through extraor-dinary measures, but in most cases, vocations to the priesthood are confirmed in more subtle ways.

Chapter Notes

"The vocation is the restless spirit of God...": Scanlon, p. 96.
"a torrent welling up from within us...": Called by God, p. 99.
"The Lord does not force or coerce us...": Ibid., p. 17.

"Vocation is free...": Raymond Hostie, SJ, *The Discernment of Vocations*, New York: Sheed and Ward, 1963, p. 19.

When Father James Keller... and f.: James Keller, *To Light a Candle*, New York: Doubleday & Company, Inc., 1963, pp. 43-44.

"Some people react to the idea of a rule..." and f.: M. Basil Pennington, *Called: New Thinking on Christian Vocation*, Minneapolis: The Seabury Press, 1983, pp. 65-69.

"Life is monotonous if it has no goal...": Fulton J. Sheen, *From the Angel's Blackboard*, Liguori, Missouri: Triumph Books, 1995, p. 37.

"Often the rule of life will need revision...": Pennington, p. 69.

eight suggestions... and f.: Sister Kathleen Bryant, RSC, *Vocations Anonymous: A Handbook for Adults Discerning Priesthood and Religious Life*, Chicago: National Coalition for Church Vocations, 1997, pp. 14-16.

"the song of praise, which shapes a life of prayer...": *Program of Priestly Formation* [75], Fourth Edition, National Conference of Catholic Bishops, 1993.

"St. Ignatius wrote the Spiritual Exercises...": Bryant, p. 35.

Father Michael Scanlon, TOR, suggests five tests...: Scanlon, p. 11.

"Lord, is it your will that I do this?" and f.: Ibid., p. 72.

... the list of authors that had the greatest influence...: *Seminarians in the Nineties, A National Study of Seminarians in Theology*, p. 4.

"Whether it was the Imitation of Christ*..."*: David Chandler, "What About Burnout?," *The Priest*, February, 1995.

"Second to service of the altar...": *Seminarians in the Nineties, A National Study of Seminarians in Theology*, pp. 12-13.

CHAPTER 5

How Do I Know This Call is From God?

"Within the last 3 months, God seems to have been stirring my heart toward His service in the priesthood. At this point I am not quite certain about whether it is truly Him calling or if it is something else." John Betts, Alexandria, Virginia

"There have been moments when I felt God calling me to the priesthood. Aside from those moments, my experience has been one of constant discernment. As the months pass, God leads me toward recognizing His will for me." Michael Cuddy, Stamford, Connecticut

"Did I ever feel dizzy, fall to the floor, and see the Queen of Heaven standing above my head? No, I never had any experience like that. I can't pinpoint a moment when I knew. I just felt like this was where I belonged. This was what God wanted me to do. It was probably there all along, so it never came upon me. I just recognized it." Michael Barone, Kenmore, New York

When Father Ragan Schriver was growing up in Tennessee, he wanted to be a priest so much that he prayed for a change in the age requirement. "You know, drop it down about 15 or 20 years," he quips. By the time he reached high school, however, he had changed his mind. "If I were ever reminded of my desire for priesthood in high school, I could change the subject easier than I could change my shoes."

After college, he began working toward a doctorate, and held several positions in family therapy and teaching. "I felt so happy and very fulfilled," he recalls. "I think that any insecurity I had about making a career for myself was gone. Yet, something was really missing."

Thoughts of the priesthood resurfaced. He talked several times with Bishop Anthony J. O'Connell of Knoxville and with Father John Artis, Vocation Director for the Paulists. But he remained unsettled and uncertain.

"One day while driving home after work, I decided to drop by the chancery office to see if I could talk to the bishop," Father Schriver recalls. "In exasperation, I told Bishop O'Connell that I wished God still made burning bushes and, in that way, would just tell me what to do. We both had a good chuckle out of that."

Later that evening, Father Schriver stopped at his parents' house. His mother, who knew nothing about his conversation with the bishop, showed him a card that had come in the mail that day. "I'm sure she wondered why my mouth dropped open," he recalls. "But there in her hand was a picture of a burning bush!"

Just as God calls each person to the priesthood in a way that is unique, the understanding that this was truly a call from God can come in different ways. In a recent survey of seminarians, some reported experiences that were "so personal that they did not feel comfortable revealing them." Most of the others indicated that it was a combination of experiences and events. "No light on the way to Damascus," one wrote, "however, numerous encounters with the glory of Our Lord."

Some people maintain that you will never have complete certainty that God is calling you to the priesthood:

"I'll be starting my second year in the seminary, and the one thing my spiritual director has emphasized is that we'll NEVER know for sure. We each need to go on what feels right in our hearts." BKL, Birmingham, Alabama

Others disagree:

"There is a deep knowing that we sometimes try to hide or snuff out. If you are being called, you know it." Father Brian McSweeney, New York, New York

Is one side right and the other side wrong? Not really. They are probably looking at this idea of "knowing" from two different perspectives. The late Bishop Fulton J. Sheen explained that there are two kinds of truth: "An *outer* truth is one we master; e.g., the distance of the sun from the earth. An *inner* truth is one that masters us; e.g., God is merciful to the penitent. Outer truths of physics and chemistry come to us without desire, sorrow, pity, or emotion. Inner truths carry some emotion with them and influence behavior."

The conviction that God is calling you to the priesthood will probably not come as an "outer" truth. You may never have absolute certainty in the same way that you know that one plus one equals two. The best you can hope for is a level of sureness that comes in recognition of "inner" truth.

For some people, this sense of certainty comes through a series of events and circumstances:

"I knew that God was calling me and that He continues to call me through various signs in my life, which I sometimes call 'coincidences.' What do I mean? Well, it's sort of like thinking about an old friend and then unexpectedly seeing that same friend just a few minutes later. God has communicated to me in this way. God has shown me things and hinted that I should pursue the priesthood. The priesthood makes sense to me because I believe I have the gifts necessary. I have a good speaking voice. I am very friendly. I love the Church, and I consider myself to be reasonably intelligent. So you might say that the combined influence of both 'coincidence' and realizing my own gifts and abilities has led me to where I am today. This has been a process, not a single event." Nicholas Zientarski, Smithtown, New York

Others experience a single moment of truth that seems to confirm and validate their vocation:

"If I could point to the one vital turning point it was a conversation I had with a woman I had been dating for a while. I told her that I thought God was calling me to priesthood or religious life. It was the first time I had said that to anybody. Before I had always said, 'I am thinking about it, but I'm not sure.' This was a crucial turning point for me. I felt amazing peace and joy. She said, 'I love you very much, but I don't think you are supposed to marry me.' Both of us just ended up laughing and talking. The whole time we were immersed in the Holy Spirit. Now, I look back to that and I say that I know for sure. It was just so evident." Philip Hurley, Baltimore, Maryland

Some say that they struggled with the decision over a long period of time:

"For years, I would think about the priesthood and investigate different groups, always to be convinced that I lacked a vocation. Since a vocation is time-connected, I believe I was right. Something changed about two years ago. I became calm about my secular career options and became content with the prospect of life as a Christian layman; therefore, I could begin to consider a response to religious life as a free choice." Dan Bettendorf, Grand Coteau, Louisiana

Some admit that they have never felt complete certainty:

"Even upon ordination I was not one hundred percent sure.
But, once you make your decision you have to live that out.
I have chosen this. I think God helped me to choose this,
and I believe God is helping me to say yes every single day.
Was there one defining moment? No! Do I feel like I said
yes? Yes! Today, I woke up and thought about how yes-
terday was a good day. I learned something new about
being a priest. I try to pick out what that is. What did I
learn? What did I do? How did I serve in a special way that
made being a priest make sense in my own life and in the
life of the Church?" Father Jim Bastian, Amherst, New York

Some find certainty in the ordinary progression of events:

"I went to see an priest from India who was living in my
parish. I asked him, 'How do I know this is the right thing
to do?' I had read all these biblical stories about calls in the
Scripture and nothing phenomenal had happened to me.
He said, 'I had the very same question when I was in the
seminary. I talked to the rector and he told me, "You will
take your exams and you will pass. You will continue in
your courses and graduate. You will be assigned certain
ministries, you will do them, and you will enjoy them. Then
you will ask the bishop if he will ordain you, and he will
say yes. Those are the kinds of signs you can expect. They
are very ordinary."' That made a lot of sense to me. If you
find that you don't like it, or if you're not passing, or you're
not getting along with people, you begin to realize that
maybe this is not the right thing." Father Ron Pecci, OFM,
Holy Name Province

Sometimes, a defining moment comes after a commitment to
the priesthood has already been made:

"It wasn't until after I was ordained that I had a confirmation that this really was without a doubt what God wanted
me to do. I was 30-years-old and I made a Cursillo. At the
end of the weekend, I had a real confirmation that the

priesthood was for me — not that I ever questioned it before that — but I felt this was it. It was almost like the sacrament of Confirmation." Monsignor John Madsen,
Depew, New York

While there is no quantitative way to measure or validate
whether someone has been called by God to the priesthood, there
are built-in safeguards to the decision-making process. What many
people don't realize is that a vocation to the priesthood is not your
decision alone. Both the person and the Church must recognize the
vocation as an authentic call from God.

"For priests, the authenticity of the vocation is canonically
assured only when the man is accepted by the bishop for sacerdo-
tal ordination; for religious, it is only when the superior of a religious congregation accepts the final vows of the candidate," notes
Father Joseph H. Fichter, SJ. "Objectively, then, in accordance with
canon law, it is ordination or the official acceptance of vows that
guarantees the validity of the vocation."

Bishop Paul Loverde agrees. "When you have those two equa-
tions — the person, after all that formation and training feels called,
and the bishop confirms that call — there's certainty," he insists.

Father Paul Koetter, former Vocation Director for the Archdiocese of Indianapolis, describes this process of confirmation as a
verification of both internal and external signs that someone has a
vocation to the priesthood.

"Internally, the candidate senses a desire to move toward
priesthood," he explains. "The person feels an attraction which is
difficult to explain. Externally, the *calling* needs to have signs that
this direction makes sense. These signs are objective and can be
pointed out. For example, the person enjoys doing retreat work or
visits a nursing home once a week. He might give counsel to many
friends or be president of the parish board of education. These talents are much easier to judge than the internal process of *feeling called*.
Most potential seminarians who walk through my door believe they
are being called by God (internal). Some of them also express awareness of the visible evidence of the call (external). It takes time to

help a person see the importance of external verifications of the internal feeling."

> "I was praying in front of the Blessed Sacrament and I asked God to help me be what he wants me to be. For the first time I felt like I knew that the priesthood was what I was supposed to do. It scared me, but I found my answer. At least I think it's my answer because you cannot be this certain before going into the seminary. I think this is what I'm supposed to do. If I'm wrong then I have a feeling God will stop me." Jason Vidmar, Davenport, Iowa

"Discernment is a gradual process," explains Father Richard Siepka, Rector of Christ the King Seminary in East Aurora, New York. "Eventually you come to a sense of peace with yourself and you begin to feel that this is the right thing. Sure there are some questions, and some things are not quite as comfortable as other things, but it all comes down to: Is this what God is calling me to do? I firmly believe that God doesn't call us to be miserable. He calls us to find happiness and fulfillment. If you feel happy and fulfilled in the process, then it is a sign that this is what God wants you to do."

Don't be startled, however, if you start to feel sure, and then doubts, fear, and feelings of unworthiness suddenly crash down. That's part of the process, too.

Chapter Notes

When Father Ragan Schriver was growing up... and f.: Ragan Schriver, "Responding to the 'Burning Bush,'" *The Priest*, October, 1996.

"so personal that they did not feel comfortable..." and f.: *Seminarians in the Nineties, A National Study of Seminarians in Theology*, 1993.

"An outer truth is one we master...": Sheen, p. 124.

"For priests, the authenticity of the vocation...": Joseph H. Fichter, SJ, "Vanishing Church Professionals," *The Crisis in Religious Vocations: An Inside View*, Laurie Felknor, ed. New York: Paulist Press, 1989, p. 102.

"Internally, the candidate senses a desire...": Rev. Paul Koetter, "Choosing Seminary: Who and Why," *Horizon*, Fall, 1991, pp. 14-15.

CHAPTER 6

Lord, I am not Worthy

"I am pretty sure that I want to be a priest, but my problem arises in the area of faith. I ask the big question of myself.... Am I strong enough??? Is my faith strong enough??? I don't feel worthy enough. If I am to be a priest, I want to be a good one — not a guy who is struggling with his own belief in the religion. Perhaps it is just a fear that I am feeling — a part of my discernment." Nicholas Zientarski, Smithtown, New York

"Even though I have considered careers as varied as law and medicine, I am reluctant to give the priesthood serious attention. I am pulled away in two directions, thinking alternately that I am not worthy of the calling or that it is not worthy of me; both fears are the fruit of pride." Bobby Jindal, Washington, DC

"I feel a calling for the priesthood, but I don't feel worthy. Can anyone give me some advice on what I can do?" John Betts, Alexandria, Virginia

Thomas Merton was only a few weeks away from entering the Franciscan novitiate when feelings of unworthiness submerged him in a kind of black hole. "I suddenly remembered who I was, who I had been," he admitted. "When I looked at myself in the light of this doubt, it began to appear utterly impossible that anyone in his right mind could consider me fit for the priesthood."

Merton was a recent convert to Catholicism. During a previous affair with a woman in England, he had fathered a child. His life was still unsettled. He suddenly began to struggle with doubts. When a Franciscan friar encouraged him to withdraw his application for the novitiate, Merton felt as if his vocation had crumbled. "There seemed to me to be no question that I was now excluded from the priesthood forever."

Thomas Merton eventually discovered his true vocation as a Trappist monk, but in the process, he had to wrestle with feelings of fear, bewilderment, and unworthiness. A recent study confirms that this kind of experience is common. When asked what factors might cause someone to hesitate about pursuing a vocation, 57 percent of those surveyed felt that they were not that religious; and 35 percent admitted that they didn't feel worthy.

> "In order to respond to God's call, I don't think it's enough to just recognize that he is calling you. As we can see in the calling of Moses, Jeremiah, and many others, there are many reasons to take a step back: the fear of not being able to make it, the fear of loneliness, and doubts of all sorts and kinds." Sandro Salvucci, Fermo, Italy

Father Vincent O'Malley, CM, witnessed this phenomenon frequently during his 13 years in vocation-formation ministry for the Vincentians. "There is that sense of not being worthy and not being able," he explains. "I used to look for feelings of inadequacy or unworthiness as a sign of a true vocation. Anyone who thinks without a doubt that he can do this vocation, reveals that he does not have a vocation."

Why? Because the reality is that no one is worthy of this call. A vocation is an invitation from God. In responding to God's call, we surrender our lives so that God can work through us.

"We have to go back in God's plan and see that God chooses who He wants to be ministers in the Church," explains Bishop Paul Loverde. "He has chosen human beings who are all unworthy. He does that, as St. Paul says, so that the power of God will shine through and nothing we do will really be our own. We are all unworthy, but God chooses us precisely because we are. No one is perfect. We all need to know that."

> "In my own experience, I've discovered that one of my weaknesses is when things get tough I want to bail out. I'm the pastor of a parish with 1,125 households. I'm not gifted as an administrator or as a fund raiser. Frankly, when I went to the parish, I said, 'Okay, Lord, you put me here. You knew what I was when you put me here. You know I'm not a good administrator. That's your problem. I will do everything I can to assist you.' I made a promise to Our Lord that since He put me in this parish, I will stay there until He makes it clear that He wants me to move elsewhere. That's the only way I can protect myself from the human tendency that I have to get out when things get rough. My lack of skills is not important. God will use whatever He has given me." Father Bob Fagan, Allentown, Pennsylvania

One skill that many men fear they lack is the gift of public speaking:

> "A priest told me that if fear of speaking is the only thing stopping me from being a priest, I should explore that more deeply. 'But don't wait until you are a great public speaker before you start to study for the priesthood,' he added. 'You are not going to have it all together even when you become a priest. There are still going to be limiting factors that you are going to struggle with.'
> It took me three years before I felt comfortable speaking in front of people and that was with a lot of work and training in the seminary. It is still something that I struggle with even after being ordained for a couple of years. To have those limitations doesn't mean that you can't be a priest. I

came to realize that the other priests around me also have limitations. They all have things they are growing in and out of." Father Jim Bastian, Amherst, New York

Father Richard Rohr, OFM, believes that acknowledging our fears and limitations is an important factor in enabling us to serve others without being arrogant or judgmental. "God calls all of you to take the path of inner truth," he notes, "that means taking responsibility for *everything* that's in you: for what pleases you and for what you're ashamed of, for the rich person inside you and for the poor one. Francis of Assisi called this, 'loving the leper within us.' If you learn to love the poor one within you, you'll discover that you have room in you for others, for those who are different from you, for the least among your brothers and sisters."

"One of the hardest hurdles is to get to a point where you can actually imagine yourself as a priest. I think that is hard for many. It was for me." Mark Mossa, Grand Coteau, Louisiana

For many men today, another difficulty lies in their fear of making a permanent commitment. In a recent study, 69 percent of the young people interviewed feared they might not be capable of making a lifelong commitment.

"It stems from the fear of pain," says Father Emile Briere. "There can be no fidelity to any state in life — marriage, the single life, or the religious life — without the acceptance of pain and joy. The two go together. Remember what Jesus said: 'Anyone who does not take up his cross and follow me cannot be my disciple' (Lk 14:27). You take up the cross and then the joy comes. But all over the Western world, the message is materialism and sensualism. We want all our senses gratified. The world tell us that's what life is about. Well, that's a lie. What life is all about is love. True love is following Jesus Christ, accepting his cross, and discovering his truth."

Another concern faced by men considering the priesthood is the purity of their intentions. On one hand they may be convinced that they want to serve God and help other people, but they fear that maybe there is some hidden agenda in their psyche that draws them toward the priesthood for other reasons.

> "I hope there's not some psychological reason why I'm going into the priesthood. Some people say that maybe it's because you don't think you could find a woman to dedicate herself to you for life or because you don't think you would be a good father. I try to disregard those things because I don't believe my calling is coming from me. I believe it's coming from God." Raymond Barrett, Rochester, New York

Father Heinrich Timmerevers, Vice Rector of the Theological Seminary of Münster, Germany, notes that, in most cases, the motives for wanting to become a priest are authentic. "Youth are found to demonstrate a passion for the Gospel and for the person of Jesus Christ, a desire to live for God, and a commitment toward one's fellow human beings and toward the Church," he explains.

On the down side, however, Father Timmerevers acknowledges that some men choose the priesthood to fill an unconscious need for recognition, or to discover their identity, or as a means of finding in the Church personal support, companionship, attention and esteem.

Father Albert DiIanni, SM, Vocation Director for the Marists, recalls talking to a young man who told him, "If I become a Jesuit, I could do this, this and this. But if I become a Capuchin, I could have this, this and this. If I became a Marist, I could do this, this and this."

"This went on for three or four sessions," Father DiIanni recalls. "On the fifth session, I said, 'You appear to be having trouble making a decision so I'm going to help you. You can't become a Marist.' The reason I said that is because I felt he was all involved in himself and what he was going to get out of it instead of thinking about what he was going to do for God or other people."

"Nobody enters ministry with totally pure motives," admits

Monsignor John Madsen. "At some point you have to deal with these issues."

> "I thought priests followed Jesus and made mistakes. I did not know it was a mistake to think all priests follow Jesus. There are indeed some who follow power. And they are a disappointment." Father Richard Bowers, Milton, Massachusetts

Marie Theresa Coombs and Francis Kelly Nemeck, OMI, believe that all of these things come to light eventually. "We see how complex our motivations were in originally committing ourselves to God through a particular lifestyle or ministry. Along with a degree of sincerity, we discover many other influences upon our decision-making: selfishness, woundedness, misguided choices, hidden agendas, etc. Yet, we realize that God incorporated all that inner poverty into the formation of our vocation. The gentle silence of the Lord enlightens us with truth. That truth in turn reduces us to silence before Yahweh. It leaves us contemplative in God's loving embrace."

"One thing I am quite afraid of is my past sinfulness." M.H.

Letting go of your past and believing in God's mercy is an essential step in the process. "What's done is done and best forgotten," wrote Archbishop Daniel Buechlein, OSB, Father Howard P. Bleichner, SS, and Father Robert Leavitt, SS. "Self-accusation is a ball and chain to past troubles. Making a break with the past requires a strong act of the will. To be successful, it must be linked to current interests so that attention is anchored to the present. But clearly, a short memory on old troubles is a key ingredient for happy living."

Father Emile Briere, who has counseled many men discerning priesthood, agrees: "The seven capital vices and original sin are active in all of us," he explains. "When we look at ourselves that way, we feel guilt or shame. We become discouraged by our lack of holiness and lack of love for other people. But we can't despair. We have to move away from our own sinfulness into the mercy of God. We must say to ourselves, 'To hell with all of that! God is my Savior!'"

"I kept trying to get my life together on my own, but I failed miserably. I was trying to make myself good enough so that God would accept me. One evening I was feeling very down. I remembered that my mom had given me some audio tapes to listen to. I decided to listen to one called 'The Christian Vision.' It was a priest talking about the God of Christianity. He said, 'If the God you know doesn't love you just as you are, not as you should be, but with all of your faults, failings and sins, then you don't know the God of Christianity.' I stopped the tape and said to myself, 'The God that I know hates me for what I've done.' I continued the tape, and the priest said, 'If you want to know the God of Christianity, go before a crucifix and pray for 30 minutes. Confront yourself with the greatest expression of God's love for you — that He would be willing to be tortured, whipped, beaten, humiliated, and crucified so that you could have life.'

"I didn't have a crucifix in my room, and I wasn't about to go find one. I just knelt down and started to pray. Suddenly, it was like I was there on Calvary. I could see Jesus on the cross, covered in blood, suffering in agony. I could see myself in a pit of mud, up to my neck and sinking with no way to save myself. Then Jesus reached down from the cross and pulled me up out of the mud. I could feel the sensation of a hand reaching into my heart and pulling out all the evil that I had done. I could hardly breathe. It was unlike anything I had ever experienced before. I knew that Jesus was real. I knew that He loved me. I knew that I was forgiven for everything that I had done wrong. I felt totally clean. I also realized that I had to make a decision to follow Jesus. I could feel a pull away from Jesus saying, 'No, don't do it! You'll have to give up all the things you like to do. It's not worth it.' It was like a spiritual tug-of-war. But I

was not going to go back into the mud. I decided to surrender my entire life to Jesus." Terry Donahue, Ottawa,
Ontario

Sometimes, doubts or periods of spiritual dryness descend as
you begin to draw closer to God:

"This summer I seriously doubted the actual existence of
God. I questioned my entire foundation and everything I
had lived for. I felt really lost. Then the nagging feeling
about becoming a priest came back again, and I can't deny
it anymore. I know there's a God, and I'm pretty sure I'm
supposed to be a priest." William Betzig, Hamburg, New
York

"A vocation, being a personal commitment to a particular form
of life, must grow in depth and intensity," explains Father Raymond
Hostie, SJ. "But such a growth does not proceed without jolts and
collision, and in this it follows the laws of all life. Sudden advances
are followed by periods of lull, and apparent aridity precedes flow-
ing. There is no need to worry about these vital rhythms in which
untroubled joy alternates with distressing trials."
    Sometimes, the doubts, confusion and feelings of unworthi-
ness you experience are actually temptations:

"I think that as God is leading us along one path, Satan
plants thoughts in our minds of doing something else,
which distracts us from what God is calling us to do." Phil
Hurley, Baltimore, Maryland

Sister Kathleen Bryant, RSC, suggests that the best way to
offset temptation is to do what Jesus did when he was tempted: turn
to Scripture. One of the passages she suggests is, "Here I am, Lord,
I come to do your will" (Ps 40:7-8).
    "Another temptation might be to escape God," she adds. "Re-
member the story of Jonah running off in the opposite direction
after having been called? (Jonah 1:3) Where do you run to? What
forms of escape do you take?"

"I went through some very rough times and still feel a deep
depression from them. Usually with this depression I end
up having sinful thoughts or become consumed with the
need to escape from loneliness. I know that God desires
happiness and love for me even though I tend to forget this
truth on a daily basis." L.L., Michigan

Sometimes, dealing with deep-seated pain from the past can
be more complicated than dealing with temptations. Father Paul
Koetter, former Vocation Director for the Archdiocese of Indianapolis, estimated that 40 percent of the men who come to discuss
the possibility of the priesthood struggle with troubled, broken, or
dysfunctional family backgrounds. "Obviously background influences the development of candidates, since issues relating to dis-
ruptive childhood years must first be faced before realistic questions
of vocation can be addressed," he admits. "Frequently our students
will enter into counseling during their seminary years to deal with
family-of-origin issues. I consider this process quite normal today
and commend the seminaries for providing qualified counselors for
the students."

Father Roger Vandenakker, Formation Director for the Companions of the Cross in Ottawa, agrees that psychological counseling is sometimes needed. "We also rely on the ministry of inner
healing that developed through the Charismatic Movement," he
explains. "It's an interesting combination of spiritual gifting with
modern psychological insights. It goes back through prayer to discern issues in a person's past that could be at the root of present
problems. It is like a prayer-counseling session. It combines spiritual counseling, insight, and discernment with good psychology."

In all of this, the bottom line is trust in God. God knows who
you are. God knows all of your strengths and weaknesses. If God is
calling you to the priesthood, He will give you everything you need
to make it happen. If not, God will lead you along a different path.

"The essence of our relationship with God is one of trust,"
explains Father Michael Scanlon, TOR. "He will care for us. He
will give us the grace for the moment — not for all possible future

moments. He gives the grace to begin our walk with him. We have to trust that He will give us the grace for every possible circumstance — foreseen or unforeseen — along that path."

"My advice to someone who is considering priesthood today is: Don't be afraid of failure. No one is perfect. No one can be guaranteed that they won't fail, but with the grace of God, you can pick yourself up if you do have a slip. Nobody is worthy. Nobody is a saint. We're all struggling." Father John Catoir, Paterson, New Jersey

Father Joseph Gatto agrees. "Follow the instinct of faith," he says. "Follow the instinct of your heart. Know that the Lord is calling you and will give you the grace to carry it out."

"The only thing that sustains me in the hard times of priesthood is the thought that for some reason God has asked me to do this. There are times when I've been down on myself, or laid out by a rule, or discouraged by a pastor or by someone in the parish. I've had sad nights of weeping. But I still have the conviction that God has called me to this and he will sustain me. That knowledge will keep you going." Father Ted Jost, Tonawanda, New York

Chapter Notes

"*Even though I have considered careers...*": Bobby Jindal, "In Search of a Calling," *The Priest*, October, 1996.

"*I suddenly remembered who I was...*": Thomas Merton, *The Seven Storey Mountain*, New York: Harcourt, Brace and Company, 1948, p. 296.

"*There seemed to me to be no question...*": *Ibid.*, p. 298.

When asked what factors...: CARA *Compendium of Vocations Research*, 1997, p. 56.

"*In order to respond to God's call...*": Sandro Salvucci, "The Birth of a Vocation," *Priests of the Future: Formation and Communion*, Rev. Michael Mulvey, ed., New York: New City Press, 1991, p. 83.

"*God calls all of you to take the path of inner truth...*": Richard Rohr, *Simplicity — The Art of Living*, New York, Crossroads, 1991, p. 170.

69 percent of the young people interviewed feared...: CARA *Compendium of Vocations Research*, 1997, p. 56.

"Youth are found to demonstrate a passion..." and f.: Father Heinrich Timmerevers, "Being First of All Men and Christians," *Priests of the Future: Formation and Communion*, Rev. Michael Mulvey, ed., New York: New City Press, 1991, pp. 102-103.

"We see how complex our motivations were...": *Called by Name*, p. 150.

"I thought priests followed Jesus and made mistakes...": Robert J. Bowers, "Priest tried to catch the joy as it fell," *National Catholic Reporter*, March 29, 1996.

"What's done is done and best forgotten...": Howard P. Bleichner, SS, Daniel Buechlein, OSB, Robert Leavitt, SS, *Celibacy for the Kingdom, Theological Reflections and Practical Perspectives*.

"A vocation, being a personal commitment...": Hostie, p. 132.

Sister Kathleen Bryant, RSC, suggests... and f.: Bryant, p. 13.

"Obviously background influences the development of candidates...": Rev. Paul Koetter, "Choosing Seminary: Who and Why," *Horizon*, Fall, 1991, p. 12.

"The essence of our relationship with God...": Scanlon, p. 48.

CHAPTER 7

What Kind of Priest Should I be?

"I am wondering whether my call is to the diocesan priesthood or to a religious order. I know I have some calling, but I need to know if someone has good experience in helping discern these areas." Brandon Darling, Illinois

"From the beginning, I have clearly believed that if I were to be a priest, the diocesan route seemed more natural. I explored the religious orders, but found none to my liking." James W.J. Stroud, Henderson, Texas

"I didn't ever feel a big draw to the diocesan priesthood. My first thought was being Franciscan, and later came thoughts about the Jesuits. Without going into great detail, my discernment has led me to seek entrance into the Society of Jesus." Phil Hurley, Baltimore, Maryland

From the time Father Ron Cafeo was a little boy, he felt called to some kind of life within the Church. When he was in elementary school, he went to a Jesuit-run summer camp. "I must have expressed an interest because I went with my parents to talk to the Jesuits about a vocation. I have no clear recollection of the interview except walking out of there with the distinct impression that I wasn't smart enough to be a priest."

In high school, Father Ron began to think that maybe he was being called to a vocation with the French Christian Brothers. He entered their novitiate and stayed for three years. "At some point I saw that everyone was interested in a career," he recalled. "They were honing themselves in as teachers. I thought, 'That's not for me.' So I left."

During his college years, he watched what diocesan priests did, and that life didn't appeal to him, either. "So I pushed the idea of a vocation out of my head," he admits.

A few years later, he visited Madonna House, a Catholic community in Combermere, Ontario, which trains men, women and priests to serve the poor under promises of poverty, chastity and obedience. "I remember my first day there," Father Ron recalls. "It was hot, and I was weeding beans at the farm. At the end of the day, we went to Mass. The celebrant was one of the guys who had been in the bean field with me. I didn't know he was a priest until that moment, and I thought: 'It might be possible for me to be a priest in this context.'"

Father Ron's experience is not unique. For many men, there is a long process of searching before they find the place where God is leading them.

Father David Reinders of Casa Grande, Arizona spent three years in a Benedictine monastery, and then left. During the next ten years, he worked in parishes and taught in Catholic high schools. When he decided to enter the seminary again, he chose the diocesan priesthood because he saw a great hunger among people in parishes for a deeper spirituality. "I think God raises up people at different times in different ages to assume the roles they are called to do."

The choice between a religious community and the diocesan priesthood is a very big decision. "They have different lifestyles, different ministries, different opportunities," explains Father Vincent O'Malley, CM.

Generally speaking, a diocesan priest serves people in a particular diocese. He may be assigned full time to a parish, or he might do weekend work at a parish and hold another job during the week, such as teaching, counseling, social work, retreat work, hospital chaplaincy, or head of a diocesan department. At ordination, a diocesan priest makes a promise of obedience to the bishop and a promise of celibacy. Since diocesan priests do not take a vow of poverty, they assume responsibility for their own personal finances. They are paid a salary by the diocese. They can own their own car, keep bank accounts, and inherit or purchase real estate.

> "I like to proudly share that the diocesan priesthood is the oldest form of priesthood. We were founded and rooted in the disciples that Jesus called." Father Dennis Schmitz, Vocation Director, Archdiocese of Kansas City, Kansas

To become a diocesan priest, many dioceses require a college degree with a concentration in philosophy. If you don't have the required courses, you may enter what is called a pre-theology program for a year or two before you enter the theologate or major seminary.

A priest in a religious community takes vows of poverty, chastity, and obedience. Whatever salary they earn from teaching, chaplaincy, pastoral ministry or other work is turned over to the community. The type of work they do will depend on how the Holy Spirit guided the founder of the community.

> "We Dominicans continue to draw on our origins and the charism of St. Dominic in order to serve our calling as preachers of the Gospel. While the preaching apostolate remains the chief commitment of the Order, that task is supplemented by numerous other ministries." Father Hank Groover, OP, Southern Province of St. Martin de Porres, Miami, Florida

Likewise, Augustinian spirituality is rooted in St. Augustine; Franciscans try to emulate St. Francis of Assisi; Jesuits follow St. Ignatius Loyola; and Vincentians shape their lives according to the life and teachings of St. Vincent de Paul. The Redemptorists follow St. Alphonsus Liguori. The Claretians follow St. Anthony Claret. The Trinitarians model their lives on St. John De Matha's vision of freedom and justice in a world of captivity and oppression.

Some religious communities, such as the Trappists, are contemplative, which means they live and work in a monastery where their main focus is on a life of prayer and contemplation. Some religious communities, such as the Maryknolls, who work i foreign countries, and the Glenmary priests, who work in ru' America, are missionaries.

Most of the other religious communities are a mix of active apostolates, community life, and prayer. The Society of St. Paul, for instance, works in the field of publishing and communications. The Claretians are committed to collaborative ministry with lay people and other religious communities as a way of bringing God's love to others. The Redemptorists are known as "apostles of conversion" because they bring the good news of redemption to the poor and abandoned. The Josephites are an interracial and intercultural community whose sole apostolate focuses on evangelization to African Americans. The Paulists are known for their work in evangelization, reconciliation, and ecumenism. The Salvatorians are committed to responding to the needs of people in thirty countries around the world so that "all may come to know the Savior." The Spiritans minister in 57 countries to the oppressed, the disadvantaged, and the poor, who have not heard the Gospel message.

To become a priest in a religious community, you would first enter into a postulancy or applicant program for a year or two. This would give you the opportunity to live and work in the community. The next stage is usually a novitiate. The length of the novitiate varies, but it is usually a year or two. During this time, you will continue your discernment process, learn more about the community members, and enter more deeply into their spirituality. At the end of the novitiate, you will take temporary vows and start your seminary training. Where you attend the seminary, and whether you live at the seminary or in a house of formation off-campus, will depend on the community. Eventually, you will take permanent vows and be ordained.

> "I live in a house of formation for the Companions of the Cross with ten people — three priests and seven seminarians. I get up at either 5:40 or 6:40 a.m. depending on whether or not I plan to take my personal prayer time before or after our community prayer at 7:00 a.m. After breakfast, I walk to classes at Dominican College. After classes, I may stay at the library a bit or head back for lunch. During the afternoons, I do my studying, weekly chores, sports, etc. We do our own cooking, teaming up in pairs to cook about once a week. On Fridays, there is no scheduled meal because it is a day of fasting. Just before dinner we gather for Evening Prayer for 15 minutes. After dinner, a few of us are assigned to clean-up. At 7:00 p.m. there is Mass next door at St. Mary's parish. At 9:00 p.m., around five or six of us meet in the chapel for an evening Rosary to close the day. After that I usually read for a bit and go to bed around 10:30 p.m." Terry Donahue, Ottawa, Ontario

The breakdown of religious versus diocesan priests has changed over the past 30 years. In 1969, 60 percent were diocesan and 39 percent religious. By 1993, 74 percent were diocesan and 25 percent religious.

> "The choice of vocation ministry is about the grace of the Spirit. It has to do with how you respond to the call that you were given and what your opportunities are. If a guy never ran across a religious and didn't know about religious life, he would probably be a diocesan priest. If he grew up in a parish or went to school where religious men served in the parish, and he heard about the saint or the Order, he's more likely to join. This is the way the Spirit works." Father Paul Golden, CM, Niagara University

As a college student at St. Bonaventure University, Father Ron Pecci, OFM, admired the Franciscans. He saw them as good teachers who were down to earth, kind, welcoming, and pastoral. After graduation, Father Ron took a research job in California, but at age 25, thoughts of joining the Franciscans nagged at him. He went to see a friar, who asked, "How do you know you want to be a Franciscan?"

> "I had never read a biography of St. Francis and I knew very little about the Franciscans, except for the priests at St. Bonaventure. This friar sent me around to see as many different vocation directors as I could. I went to the Jesuits, the Carmelites, the Christian Brothers, the diocesan priests, the Claretians, the Maryknolls, but I kept coming up with Franciscans." Father Ron Pecci, OFM, Holy Name Province

An attraction to a religious community is not always a definitive sign that you should enter, however.

> "When I was growing up the priests who lived next door were Conventual Franciscans so my first contact was with a religious order. When I was young, I did some research into it. But along with the idea that I wanted to serve God as a Franciscan, there was always the idea that I wanted to serve God among the kind of people I grew up with. The diocesan priesthood seemed best for my gifts. I respect those who go elsewhere to teach or do mission work, but I always felt that I wanted to serve at home." Father Richard Siepka, Rector, Christ the King Seminary

Sometimes, a coincidence or an unexpected event will start someone thinking about a religious community that he never knew existed:

> "I was helping to organize a Charismatic conference. Father Richard MacAlear, OMI, was the main speaker. He

was the first Oblate I had ever met. I talked to him before
and after the conference. I had been praying about whether
God was calling me to the priesthood. I didn't tell him that,
but he saw it in me, and he helped me to confirm my vocation. I had been thinking about the diocesan priesthood,
but he gave me information about the Oblates. I decided
to look into it." Karl Davis, Brooklyn, New York

Some men feel attracted to a particular form of priesthood
because of an interest in a certain kind of prayer life or spirituality.
"Our vocations — ten postulants this year! — come to us usually
from contact with Carmelite spirituality," says Father Michael Dodd,
OCD, a Discalced Carmelite from Brighton, Massachusetts. "They
have read St. Teresa of Avila, St. John of the Cross, Brother
Lawrence of the Resurrection, St. Thérèse of Lisieux, etc. Or they
were encouraged by Carmelite priests, nuns or members of our secular order."

Some are attracted to religious life because of the community
and ministry:

"When I was young we moved a lot. We were poor. My
family was never close. After high school, I spent three
years studying for the diocesan priesthood, but I ended up
going with the Oblates. I was attracted to the community
life, the mobility, and the opportunity to help the poor —
not by giving them handouts — but by teaching them and
helping them to pull themselves up." Alec Bosse, Buffalo,
New York

Sometimes a person will decide to enter the diocesan seminary, and it isn't until after ordination that he begins to wonder if
he was called to religious life:

"After I had been ordained for seven years, I started looking for a more vibrant community life and theological study
as a way to get closer to God. I inquired into a number of
religious communities that accept priests. I entered the

postulancy for the Dominicans, but at the end of that period of discernment, I returned to the diocese. I realized
that God wasn't calling me to that life." Father Don
Guglielmi, East Haven, Connecticut

Before you begin to investigate the diocesan priesthood or a
religious community, it's a good idea to take a personal inventory
of your strengths and weaknesses, your likes and dislikes, your gifts,
talents, and personal preferences in terms of prayer, community
living, and ministry. Sister Kathleen Bryant, RSC, suggests that you
list the following words on a sheet of paper: Hermit, Monk, Parish
Priest, Priest in a Religious Community, Missionary Priest.

"Now spontaneously write one word associations for each
category," she says. "Without censoring, jot down any images, feelings, or descriptive phrases about that particular vocation. For example, under 'missionary' you may respond: adventurous, challenging, difficult, poor, dangerous. Under 'hermit' you might write:
lonely, too quiet, far removed, prayerful, penitential. Again, these
are only personal reactions and not necessarily the reality for all
people."

Once you have your list of talents and your word associations,
you can begin to narrow down the kind of priesthood that you
might want to investigate.

"I felt myself called to religious life. I knew of the Jesuits as
educators and writers, both of which were career goals I
had set for myself long before priesthood became a factor.
As I learned more about the Jesuits, I found not only their
apostolates, but their entire spirituality very much attractive to me. I had long been drawn to contemplative spirituality, but was also convinced that my life must be an active one in the world. The Jesuit life of 'contemplation in
action' was exactly what I was looking for." Mark Mossa,
Grand Coteau, Louisiana

"One thing people sometimes say is that religious communities have a spirituality and diocesan priests don't," notes Father Ron

Pecci, OFM. "That's not true. We both have spiritualities. We all serve the people of God. We all proclaim the kingdom of God. I think the biggest distinctions between diocesan priesthood and religious communities are practical things. In the secular priesthood, you can pick your locality. You can stay close to your family. You're able to handle your own financial resources. With the vow of poverty in a religious community, you let go of those things. It is unlikely in religious life that you will move up the ecclesiastical ladder. In a religious community, you could be at the top of the administration, but you don't have a position of leadership forever. You always have to fall back into the ranks after six or nine or twelve years. It's more egalitarian, more fraternal, because you know you're going to move back down."

> "I spoke to the Jesuits and the Vincentians. In the end the reason that I became a diocesan priest had to do with wanting to be in the trenches of the parish. I wanted to touch families. I wanted to help couples prepare for marriage. I wanted to baptize their children. I wanted to help kids get confirmed and administer the sacraments. I'm a natural teacher in many ways, but I didn't want to teach full time. I'll do my share of teaching and my share of administration as a parish priest, but I just wanted to be there touching lives on a parish level. That was important to me." Father Ted Jost, Tonawanda, New York

You can begin to investigate the diocesan priesthood and different religious communities by looking at vocation directories, subscribing to a vocation magazine, or reviewing web pages for various dioceses and religious communities on the internet.

> "The internet is especially helpful these days as you can access a number of sites which promote vocations without feeling pressured or pushed." Mark Mossa, Grand Coteau, Louisiana

As you learn more about various religious communities, you'll discover that another important element of the vocational experi-ence involves navigating your way through the conservative and liberal polarization in the Church today. "We have a Church now that is highly politicized," says Father Paul Golden, CM. "We are in tremendous tension about beliefs and practices. I think part of the vocational experience is trying to find out where you fit. A major concern when investigating a religious community would be: 'Do I fit here? Is my theology right?' I find that it is all very exciting and exhilarating, but a lot of people don't. They find it awful."

> "I knew three things about the Order I wanted to join. First, that they be devoted to the Blessed Virgin; second, that they have a special devotion to the Eucharist; and third, that they were obedient and supportive of the Pope. I found all those qualities in the Companions of the Cross, plus a fourth that I discovered was important to me also — a strong community life. Community provides the support and companionship that makes life easier." John Fletcher, Ottawa, Ontario

If a particular diocese or religious community seems interest-ing, and you want to know more, vocation directors are always willing to talk.

> "I am a vocation recruiter for the Oblates and would love to talk with anyone about any questions they may have about discernment." Father Greg Gallagher, OMI, St. Louis, Missouri

If your name ends up on a list of men discerning priesthood, you can expect a large quantity of mail. "Specifically that quantity might be in the neighborhood of a good-sized box," quips Brother Guy Jelinek, OSB, of St. Procopius Abbey in Lisle, Illinois.

> "When I was a freshman in college, I decided to send away for information on a few religious orders. Well, I really got swamped with mail." Nicholas Zientarski, Smithtown, New York

Some of the mailings will be very slick and professional. Others will be simple letters with a very basic brochure. Don't judge a religious community on the quality of its advertising. It's important to read the material carefully to see if something in the description speaks to your heart.

Some religious communities will invite you to a discernment retreat. The Legionnaires of Christ, for example, offer what they call "Test Your Call Retreats" at their novitiate in Cheshire, Connecticut, which includes Mass, talks, time for prayer and reflection, and an opportunity to meet with a spiritual director. The Redemptorists offer a discernment program called "Crossroads," which includes weekend retreats in Redemptorist retreat houses, as well as a week-long summer apostolic experience that introduces men to the Redemptorist community, their spirituality and their mission.

> "I have been on several vocational discernment retreats and visited several religious orders." Christopher Jeffrey, West Minneapolis, Minnesota

Father Albert DiIanni, SM, Vocation Director for the Marist Fathers in Framingham, Massachusetts, doesn't invite anyone to visit until he has talked to the person on the phone. "Personal contact is important," he says. "I ask how long they have been thinking about the priesthood, and then they begin to tell their story. I ask about their background and their education. If we seem to click, I ask if they would like to come down and visit with us. They live in the house for a few days and meet some of the priests. It works quite well."

A recent survey of those interested in a religious community showed that the most beneficial part of the discernment process was actually meeting members of the community, participating in their liturgies, working in their ministries, and talking to them about vocations. One candidate noted, "Visiting the community was probably the most important part of the process. I was able to see that my understanding of service and work with the poor was in line with the community's."

If you are invited to visit a religious community, Father Louis Lougen, OMI, urges you to ask critical questions. "Some guys ask things like: When could I enter? What should I bring? What courses will I need? How long will it take before I'm ordained?" he notes. "Those things are important, but they aren't really essential at this point."

If you are really serious about investigating a religious community, Father Lougen suggests that you ask:

- What is the mission of this community?
- How does this community live the vow of obedience?
- How does this community live the vow of poverty?
- What is involved in the community life?
- How does this community pray?
- Where is this community heading in the future?

If you're not ready for letters, phone calls, retreats or invitations to visit, you might want to make an initial contact with the vocation office in your own diocese.

> "I wanted to just search this out a little bit at a time. Someone pointed out where the vocation director's office was. Before that, I had no idea of how to go about this thing without opening the whole thing up." Father Kevin Creagh, CM, Niagara Falls, New York

Father Robert Wozniak, Vocation Director for the Diocese of Buffalo, admits that his primary concern is helping men become diocesan priests. "But I don't think that everyone is called to the diocesan priesthood," he concedes. "So I have to be open to listen to where their needs are going to be met and where they can use their gifts as best as possible."

Monsignor Paul Burkard agrees. "I always try to listen to what experience someone has in service to people," he says. "That's almost a natural characteristic of a diocesan priest and many religious orders. Sometimes, you get a guy who tells you about his spiritual life and how he's thought about priesthood for a long time, but he never once mentions that he has been involved in service to people or in service to the Church. You think, what kind of priesthood is this guy looking for? Then it occurs to you: He's looking for a monastery or some other kind of contemplative religious life. That's fine. That's a vocation."

> "When I talked to the Vocation Director in Brooklyn, he suggested that I not become a diocesan priest. He suggested that I look to the Jesuits." Father Benjamin Fiore, SJ, Canisius College, Buffalo, New York

Many dioceses work cooperatively with religious orders to offer days of reflection or special programs for men considering the priesthood. "We invite priests, religious, youth ministers, and people from the parishes to invite anyone interested in the diocesan priesthood or religious life to a dinner," explains Father Paul Etienne, Vocation Director for the Archdiocese of Indianapolis. "We do that several times a year in different parts of the archdiocese. The first several years, 10 percent of the people who came entered into a formation program. I think that's pretty successful. Once we get someone's name, we stay in contact on a monthly basis through a newsletter. We invite them to participate in anything else we may offer."

Sometimes, a bishop will attend these kinds of sessions:

> "Recently, I was down in Cassadaga, New York and the pastor invited 13 young men to have lunch with us. We had a wonderful conversation for an hour and a half about the priesthood. I was encouraged by the conversation, the questions, the comments. I believe the priesthood is truly a great way to spend one's life. I believe God is calling, but sometimes we don't extend the invitation frequently enough." Bishop Henry J. Mansell, Diocese of Buffalo

Father Stephen DiGiovanni, Vocation Director for the Diocese of Bridgeport, Connecticut invites young men considering both diocesan priesthood and religious orders to visit the house of discernment at St. John Fisher Seminary in Stamford. "It has helped nearly 200 men during the past eight years to discern God's will," he explains. "Most have gone on to the seminary; 27 have been ordained so far; some have gone into religious life; others have discovered God's call to the married life or to single life."

Many dioceses host discernment prayer groups on a weekly or monthly basis:

> "There are three or four vocation discernment groups that meet regularly in the Diocese of Orange. Some priests have dedicated themselves to a weekly Holy Hour before the Blessed Sacrament to pray for vocations and those in discernment. They invite prospective candidates to join them for the hour and for some sharing time afterward. It's pretty informal, but those who are doing it are convinced that sacrificing time and prayer are the only real ways to get the grace flowing." Father Chris Heath, Tustin, California

After a while, most men discover that their discernment begins to move them in a particular direction. "Certainly, when you're making a decision, you are opening a door and closing a door," admits Father Paul Golden, CM. "There's always that desire to keep all the doors open, but you can't keep all the doors open forever. You have to close some doors."

> "I liked the Dominicans very much, and I thought I might be called to be a Dominican. I also checked a couple different dioceses. After two years of discerning, I realized I wasn't getting anywhere fast. I went to see a priest. He told me, 'Tim, your vocation is not to search, your vocation is to live.' He was the impetus or the spark to make me decide what God was calling me to do, and I decided it was the diocesan priesthood. It took a little pushing because I

was afraid to make the jump. I'm glad that priest pushed me." Tim Bohen, West Seneca, New York

Paul MacNeil, a seminarian from the Diocese of St. Catharine's, Ontario, agrees: "At some point you have to make a decision one way or the other," he says. "There are many decision points like that along the way, and at each point, you're going to have to choose one way or the other. The truth is that you shouldn't be afraid of those decisions because you can't lose. If you go to the seminary or enter a religious order, that's fine. If you decide not to become a priest, that's fine, too. But you have to make the decision at some point."

It's usually during these decisive moments that another difficult question arises: "What will my family and friends think of me if I do this?"

Chapter Notes

"I think God raises up people...": Arthur Jones, "Writing icons part of journey to priesthood," *National Catholic Reporter*, September 12, 1997.

In 1969, 60 percent were diocesan and 39 percent religious...: Seminarians in the Nineties, A National Study of Seminarians in Theology, p. 3.

"Now spontaneously write one word associations...": Bryant, p. 98.

A recent survey of those interested in a religious community... and f.: Patrice J. Touhy, "What candidates think of the discernment process," *Horizon*, Convocation Issue, 1996, p. 32.

CHAPTER 8

What do I tell my Family and Friends?

"I am discerning whether or not to enter the seminary. My parents are not helping with the decision and are not making it any easier." Jason Vidmar, Davenport, Iowa

"My family reacted surprisingly well. I expected considerable dismay, or at least mild amusement, but everyone was very respectful and supportive. Most surprising was the response of old friends and drinking buddies who were uniformly pleased and happy for me." Daniel Bettendorf, Grand Coteau, Louisiana

"My mother, who is a practicing Catholic, was very happy. My father was not very happy. He said that he will support my decision, but that I should consider it carefully. The rest of my family was speechless. I did not hear any comments from them." Javier Tirado, Miami, Florida

On several occasions, Father George Bergin, SVD, vocation director for the Divine Word Missionaries, talked at length on the telephone to a young man, who expressed an interest in becoming a priest. Finally, they arranged to meet in person at the young man's home. When Father Bergin arrived, the young man's father answered the door.

"Who are you?" the father asked. "Why are you here?"

"This young man had never told his parents that he was thinking about the priesthood or that he had talked with me," Father Bergin recalls.

Ever since this embarrassing episode, Father Bergin always asks potential candidates: "Who knows that you're thinking about this?"

Some people dread the thought of telling their family and friends that they are considering a vocation to the priesthood:

> "I am sure of two things: Throughout my life God has allowed me to learn things that will make me a good caring person, and that I am called to serve Him as a diocesan priest. I have told very few people of my intentions. The hardest part will be to tell my parents. I guess I'm a little behind where I'd like to be." T.R., Binghamton, New York

There is no official timetable for when you should begin to tell other people that you are discerning a vocation to the priesthood. For some, it happens early in the discernment process because they want support and encouragement:

> "My parents always knew because I talked about it from the time I was little. They were very supportive, but they didn't push it. I never had the feeling that if I didn't do it, it would be a terrible disappointment to them. I always got a lot of support and encouragement from my two older brothers. There was never anyone in the family who said, 'How could you do that?'" Father David LiPuma, Buffalo, New York

Some seek out selected people to tell:

> "In high school I kept it a secret. Eventually, I told more and more people, but I only told people who I knew would support me. As a result, I got a lot of support from my friends." William Betzig, Hamburg, New York

Others wait until after they have been accepted into a religious community or a diocesan formation program:

"When I decided to go into the seminary, I shared it with very few people. I didn't even tell my parents about it. Finally, a friend said, 'You've got to tell your mother. She can't find out about this from someone else.' So I went home and announced to the family what I was going to do. My mother's jaw dropped. She didn't say a word. She just walked out of the room, and we heard the vacuum cleaner running. Later she told me that she was crying." Father Ted Jost, Tonawanda, New York

The worst case scenario unfolds when parents find out from someone else:

"I am close to my brother, who is four years younger. I started discussing the priesthood with him almost immediately after I started thinking about it. He told my mom before I could get to her. She was very upset — almost coming to tears. My dad was also very 'concerned.' He asked many questions, relating mainly to my well-being and 'Who's going to take care of you?' kind of things. Now, months later, they are all okay about it. I think they all just want me to be happy. They've come to understand that I can be happy as a priest." Nicholas Zientarski, Smithtown, New York

A negative reaction from parents is more common than you might suspect. Research shows that when parents of young people were asked whether they had encouraged their children to consider a vocation, 48 percent said no, and an additional 19 percent felt strongly that a parent should not encourage vocations.

"It seems that there's been a culture shift that has made the priesthood an unattractive vocation," observes Father James Hennesey, SJ. "Even my nephew, who has two sons — ages five and three — told me, 'I wonder how I'll advise them if they want to become priests. I'm frightened by that commitment.' I said, 'Scott, what about your commitment to Doreen and to them? Your commitment is every bit as serious and every bit as daunting.' He hadn't thought of it that way."

A recent study reveals that 70 percent of the parents interviewed expressed concern that their children would not be happy in the priesthood; 59 percent felt that a young man would be lonely without the intimacy and support of a spouse; 53 percent expressed a desire for grandchildren; 51 percent felt their son would be too limited as a priest; 43 percent wanted their children to achieve material success.

Mothers are more likely to emphasize grandchildren. Fathers tend to emphasize material success. Father Michael Scanlon, TOR, experienced both reactions when he told his family that he wanted to become a priest. "I am an only child," he explains. "My mother was grief-stricken at the news that she would never have grandchildren. My father, who had been divorced from my mother for many years, thought I had been brainwashed by religious fanatics. He thought I would be wasting my talents and a Harvard law degree. My mother's husband was furious at me for 'breaking your mother's heart.'"

Father Scanlon went into the seminary anyway. "Family reactions to major life decisions should ordinarily be carefully considered," he admits. "But the call from God to be a priest had been clear, strong, and consistent. It had been confirmed in many ways. And there was plenty of time to test it before it was irrevocable."

Over the next seven years, Father Scanlon watched in awe as the lives of his mother, father, and stepfather were transformed. "My mother and father both returned to the sacramental life of the Church and died as faithful Catholics," he explains. "My mother experienced an exceptional transformation; she spent her last years in the practice of habitual contemplative prayer. My stepfather, who had never been a Christian, converted and embraced the Catholic Church.... It was another sign that I was on the right course. For them, my shocking and disappointing decision became a source of

r own lives, an occasion to hear the Lord's invitation
serve Him."
.gative reaction from parents is always upsetting, but it
ُpecially unnerving if you don't expect it.

. remembered how excited my mother was when our family dentist announced that his son had decided to become
a rabbi. I thought she would feel the same way when I told
her that I wanted to be a priest, but she didn't. I had two
brothers, and my parents already had a grandson, so that
wasn't the issue. For my parents, the issue was, 'Ronald, it's
much more difficult than you think. There are so many
problems today. Are you sure you want to do this?' For the
first couple of years, they would come to visit, and my
mother would say, 'Just remember. You can always come
home if it doesn't work out.' They accepted it eventually.
Now I think if I left the priesthood, they would be shocked
and disappointed." Father Ron Pecci, OFM, Holy Name
Province

"We're finding that people in seminaries need support and
encouragement from their parents," says Bishop Paul Loverde. "Parents need to be involved. But some parents are fearful of pressuring
their sons so they step back."

"I always let my son know that I will not be disappointed
in him if he changes his mind. When I say this he thinks
that I don't believe in him. But that is not it! I wanted to be
a nun until I was in ninth grade, and then changed my mind.
I think I disappointed some family members." B.T., Arizona

When parents encourage their sons to pursue a vocation, it is
because they see the priesthood as "a satisfying, faith-based, car-
ing profession in a secular and technological world."

"In their heart of hearts, my parents were very supportive.
They were devout Catholics and they wanted me to do

what would make me happy. If the priesthood was what
God wanted me to do, then they knew it would make me
happy." Father Don Guglielmi, East Haven, Connecticut

Studies show that while parental encouragement is not the
most important factor in a man's decision to pursue a vocation, it is
important for everyone's peace of mind to strive for openness and
good communication. You have to understand that your decision
to become a priest may trigger some of your parents' fears and shatter some of their dreams. Your parents have to understand that this
is what you believe God is calling you to do. It may take a while
for all of you to work through this together.

> "I don't really talk to my parents much about my faith so
> this was really hard for them. It came as a shock. They don't
> understand. I can't say they were very supportive, but they
> did tell me that after a year of discerning and talking to
> others, if I still want to go to the seminary, they will support me. This year will be a growing time for all of us. I am
> thankful that I have them around to grow with." Jason
> Vidmar, Davenport, Iowa

Father Paul Bombadier of Ware, Massachusetts poses the following questions for men struggling with the decision of when to
tell their parents:

• What was your own internal reaction when you made the
decision to pursue the priesthood?
• For whom are you making this decision? If you are doing it
to please someone else, it is not your decision.
• How secure are you in making your own decisions? Do you
need the approval of others to get your certainty? This makes a tremendous amount of difference. If you are not sure within yourself
you will not be able to deal with opposition.
• How did you feel and what did you think about when you
started to realize that you had to tell your family?
• Can you survive emotionally without your parents' support?

"Discerning a religious vocation in today's world is a thankless task," Father Bombadier admits. "Very few people understand what you are talking about, and even those who do will concentrate on what you will 'give up,' that is, sexual intercourse. They do not see the kinds of things priests are involved in. They do not see the kind of commitments that priests make. They have no real concept that priests do not just 'give up.' Priests take upon themselves, with God's help, the lives of those they are called to serve. A good sized amount of altruism is necessary. A good sense of self is essential for survival's sake. Trying to defend the discernment that you are undergoing, as terrible as this may sound, is not something that some people can understand. It is not worth trying to convince them because then you sound a lot like you are trying to convince yourself as well. The decision to undergo this discernment and the self-knowledge and examination that it takes must come out of your life as you are living it already. It is a natural part of your personality and part of God's gift to you."

"Living some 900 miles from my family, my friends were more present to the situation. Almost without exception, they were very supportive and showed little surprise. Most were familiar with my work in youth ministry and many had been involved with or seen me at work." Mark Mossa, Grand Coteau, Louisiana

It's great when good friends affirm you, but it doesn't always work that way. "One of the biggest struggles for young men considering the priesthood is having others make fun of him or shun him," admits Father Chris Heath of Tustin, California.

"When my great uncle became a priest, it was an honor. For me, people said, 'Are you gay?' 'What's your problem?' 'Are you weird?' It was a countercultural thing for me to become a priest." Father Ted Jost, Tonawanda, New York

Sometimes, the reactions of others can be amusing:

"The overwhelming thought people had was that I was 'leaving the world.' The first time someone said that to me I burst out with, 'For God's sake, I'm not DYING!!' That broke things up quite a bit, as you may imagine. Then we got to talking about the reality of priestly life these days, and they soon realized there was no leaving the world, but because of our celibacy we throw ourselves into the world more than they ever could." Father Paul Bombadier, Ware, Massachusetts

After a while, the questions and comments can get boring:

"Most of the time you get the typical things: 'Why you?' 'You'd be a good teacher.' 'You could even be a lawyer.' 'You're good looking.' 'Don't you want to get married or have children?'" Father Joseph Gatto, East Aurora, New York

In the process, you find out who your real friends are:

"People look at you differently when you say, 'I want to dedicate my whole life to God as a priest.' I was afraid of that. I decided to get a buzz cut before I told anyone that I was going into the seminary. Some people said, 'You look like a dork.' But the people who were really my friends said, 'It looks fine. You are who you are.' Those were the same people who responded positively when I told them I was going into the seminary. It was important for me to know that the people who are my real friends supported me in whatever I was going to do." Father Jim Bastian, Amherst, New York

For Father Marvin Kitten, SJ, of New Orleans, one of the most difficult encounters was explaining to "a lovely lady from Texas Tech," that he had decided to become a Jesuit. "We were attracted to one another. I had even brought her home to meet my parents and four brothers. They all liked her. And so did I."

He decided to meet her at her dorm and just tell her the truth. He stuffed four of his favorite shirts in a paper bag as a parting gift for her. "My plan was to escape when she began to open the bag," he admits. "I'm not too good at crying scenes!"

After his ordination to the priesthood, he was assigned to a Jesuit school in Dallas. "One Sunday, I turned around and there was the young lady from Tech! She lived three blocks away with her husband and two children. She invited me to dinner and we have become lifelong friends."

When to tell people at work is another consideration. Most vocation directors suggest that you don't tell your employer until you've been accepted into a religious community or a diocesan formation program:

> "The people I worked with were shocked. Most were not Catholic, and in fact, most of them were not even Christian. My boss was Jewish. Most of the others were Asians. There was one Jamaican woman, who was a devout Christian, and she thought it was wonderful. But most of the others did not understand." Father Ron Pecci, OFM, Holy Name Province

Father Bob Couto of Nashua, New Hampshire was 44 years old and the vice president of an international corporation when he decided to enter the seminary. "My business associates thought I was crazy," he recalls "How could I give up a promising and blossoming career to be a priest? Well, I was never motivated by money. My life spanned a variety of careers — all intended to educate me in real life situations so that I could better serve God's holy people."

> "We should not strictly see the end product of our discernment as the primary finish line of it all — the point in time where we will FINALLY be working for God. We should be open to His using us as instruments at every step of the journey. So, as soon as you feel comfortable enough talking about your potential vocation, feel free to tell the whole world — literally! You never know who might be listening, and who out there might really need to hear what you have to say." David Scoma, Maitland, Florida

Once you start to tell people, you can count on getting lots of unsolicited advice:

> "When I was going off to the seminary, a nun said to me, 'Joseph, if you're going to be a priest, you be a damn good one. Otherwise, don't even bother! We have enough mediocre priests. If you're not someone who realizes that God's grace can change you, pull you, tug you, you're never going to be able to be a leader who can do that for the people of God.'" Father Joseph Gatto, East Aurora, New York

You'll also discover that some people will begin to pray for you:

> "I am convinced that the prayers of others had so much to do with my life even though they never told me about it. I am grateful for the prayers of others." Father Gilio Dipre, Erie, Pennsylvania

"You need support," admits Bishop Paul Loverde. "It may be difficult in terms of lack of parental support or the support of your friends, but you can go on. The best way to find the support you need is to go to the seminary. That's what it's for — to nurture and help discern vocations."

The problem is that you don't just go to the seminary. You have to apply for admission. In the next chapter, we'll take a closer look at what the application process involves.

Chapter Notes

Research shows that when parents of young people were asked...: CARA *Compendium of Vocations Research*, 1997, p. 72.

A recent study reveals that 70 percent of the parents... and f.: Ibid., pp. 59-60.

"I am an only child... and f.: Scanlon, pp. 65-66.

When parents encourage their sons to pursue a vocation...: CARA *Compendium of Vocations Research*, 1997, p. ix.

Studies show that while parental encouragement is not the most important factor:...: Ibid.

CHAPTER 9

Taking the Next Step ✝

"I'm 18 years old, and I've thought about a priestly vocation for a while, but until two months ago, no one ever asked me about going to the seminary. I prayed and found it's God's will that I at least go to the seminary. I think I am called further, but I'll take things one step at a time." Brendon Darling, Illinois

"I came to the Church about a year ago. I feel a calling to the priesthood. Can someone give me some advice on what I should do next?" John Betts, Alexandria, Virginia

"Do you have to decide that you want to be a priest before you go to college? How much school do you need? What do you have to do?" Dan Hunt, Williamsville, New York

During his senior year in college, the Newman Center chaplain asked the future Father Marvin Kitten, SJ, if he had ever thought of becoming a priest. Kitten brushed off the suggestion, and after graduation, he took a job with Geophysical Services, Inc. The priest at the Newman Center didn't give up. He continued to write to Kitten with the question: "How's your discernment about priesthood coming?"

"Marvin, if this priesthood stuff won't go away, maybe you'd better check it out," one of his friends suggested.

The problem was: Where to begin? "I had known only two priests in my life," Father Kitten recalls. "I liked them both, but I was not attracted to the diocesan model. The next Sunday at Mass, I noticed *America* magazine in the rack. I bought a copy."

As he flipped through the magazine he remembered reading about the Jesuits in a history course. "So I wrote to the editor of *America* and asked him where I could find a live Jesuit. He got me in contact with the Jesuit Provincial. The more I met with this good man, the more I liked what I heard, such as: 'For the greater glory of God'; 'The world is the monastery'; 'Contemplatives in action'; 'Finding God in all things'; 'Inserting oneself into the world to make a difference.' I went through the application process and I was accepted!"

Sounds simple. Actually, the process is a bit more complicated, but don't worry. There will always be people to help you along the way.

Where you begin the application process will depend on your age, your educational level, and whether you are interested in the diocesan priesthood or a religious community. There are still a few high school seminaries, but they are very rare, and many experts today advise young men to attend a regular high school. After that, you could look into the possibility of attending a college seminary.

"I wanted to go to a college seminary until I visited Wadhams Hall Seminary College in the spring of my senior year. I had never been far away from my parents. I remember feeling very lonely, very anxious. After the weekend was over, I told my parents I didn't want to go there. I applied to other colleges, but I didn't feel settled. I talked to a priest at my high school. We were walking around the horseshoe in the school driveway and I kept saying, 'I don't know what to do. Should I go?' He suggested that maybe the best thing for me would be to experience being away from home. He emphasized very clearly that if I got there and didn't like it, I could always come home. It was the best advice." Father David LiPuma, Buffalo, New York

At a college seminary (sometimes called a minor seminary), you will take 24 credit hours in philosophy, a minimum of 12 credit hours in theology, and some Latin or Greek. After graduating, you will attend the major seminary, where you will go through four more years of graduate work in theology.

"I am a seminarian at St. Mary's Seminary in Baltimore. We actually have men that fall into two categories — those with college degrees and those who are still working on their college degrees. Most men at St. Mary's received their degrees from secular schools although there are some who attended 'minor seminaries.' My undergraduate degree is a B.A. in Chemistry from the University of Colorado." B.K.L., Birmingham, Alabama

Men who start to think about the priesthood after they've already graduated from college must complete their undergraduate philosophy, religion and Latin requirements before applying to the major seminary. "You enter what is called a pre-theology program, which usually is a two-year course of studies in philosophy, Catholic theology and classical languages," explains Father Stephen DiGiovanni, Vocation Director for the Diocese of Bridgeport, Connecticut. "This gives you two years to develop your prayer life and to perfect your decision regarding the priesthood."

You might want to look into the possibility of living in a house of discernment while you attend classes at a nearby college, university or seminary. Many dioceses and religious communities have their own houses of discernment, which include daily prayer, formation, spiritual direction, workshops, retreats, and apostolic service. In Milwaukee, for instance, St. Anthony's parish runs Casa San Antonio, a house of discernment for Hispanic men who are discerning a vocation to the priesthood.

"A house of discernment offers someone the opportunity to

go through the discernment process with support from the formation staff," explains Monsignor Paul Burkard. "It basically says,
'We've got a place for you. We have people who are going to help
you. We've got other people thinking and asking the same questions. You can live here and bounce questions off of them. At the
same time, you can live a quasi-normal college life.' That is the real
value of a place like that. It is for people who are not yet ready to
step into a full blown seminary program. It gives them an opportunity to test the waters and do the thinking they need to do with
the support they need to do it. It doesn't call for a complete commitment, but it provides a wonderful taste of what that commitment will be and what seminary life will be like. I think it's one of
the most effective programs we have going today."

> "I would tell a man who is considering the priesthood to
> find a great house of discernment and apply for acceptance.
> It is certainly worthwhile to try it." Michael Cuddy, Stam-
> ford, Connecticut

Once you have obtained a bachelor's degree and the necessary background in philosophy, you can apply for admission to the
major seminary or theologate. Seminaries can be established by
dioceses or by religious communities. Sometimes seminaries and
religious communities collaborate with universities, which means
the seminary or the religious community offers formation, while
the university offers academic course work.

Requirements for admission to a college seminary, a house of
discernment or a theologate will vary depending on the diocese and
the religious community, but there are certain elements that are
common to all. Canon law, for instance, requires that before admission to a seminary you submit a copy of your parents' marriage
certificate, and your Baptism, First Communion and Confirmation
certificates.

You will be asked to complete an application form and submit letters of recommendation from your pastor, former teachers,
employers, volunteer service coordinators, etc. Most vocation di-

rectors will also ask you to write the story of your life. It doesn't have to be a definitive autobiography. Figure on about 10 typed pages detailing the key elements in your life and faith experience.

You will need transcripts from high school, college and graduate school. If you were in the military, you will need photocopies of your discharge papers. Medical and dental examinations must be arranged. You may be asked to sign release forms so medical records can be obtained.

> "I am a 43-year-old with HIV disease. I have put off the calling for nearly 30 years, and now I can no longer answer His calling. I have sent out resumes to about 35 communities. I have been getting a lot of 'no' on medical reasons. But I've had some possibles. I continue to pray and meditate. It seems to help me cope." D.F., Chicago, Illinois

Each diocese and religious community will have specific requirements in terms of health and medical history. They are all looking for men who have the health and the stamina to do what priesthood demands. Some are very strict in their requirements. Others are more lenient. Sister Kathleen Bryant, RSC, tells candidates that they can stop the application at any point without disclosing information that they might prefer to keep private. "For example," she says, "if your medical exam reveals that you are HIV positive and if there is a policy of not accepting HIV candidates, you could stop the application process without disclosing that information. Inform the doctor, before the lab results are sent back to the vocation director, that you are not continuing the process."

> "I am 48 years old and the thought of the priesthood has been with me since I was a kid. I wrote to several religious orders, and I'm getting very nice letters that essentially say I'm too old." R.M., Denver, Colorado

Policies on a candidate's age will vary depending on the diocese or religious community. Some dioceses and religious communities set an upper age limit. Others see older candidates as bring-ing rich and varied backgrounds to the priesthood. The major con-cern is whether or not a candidate has become set in his ways. Vocation directors will look for indications of flexibility and will-ingness to adapt. Some people are surprised to learn that a few semi-naries actually specialize in "second career vocations."

> "I began to look around for seminaries where the policies were more lenient in the acceptance of older men. I was informed about Holy Apostles College and Seminary by a woman who worked in a vocation director's office. I called the information number listed for the seminary. When my call was transferred to the Director of Admissions, I re-ceived a recorded message. I left my telephone number never expecting to hear from them again. In about twenty minutes I received a call from a delightful person who as-sured me that I was just the kind of person the seminary was in operation to support." Roger L. Depue, Cromwell, Connecticut

"We have all types of seminarians from all over the country," says Father Raymond J. Halliwell, MSA, Director of Admissions at Holy Apostles College and Seminary. "In the last six years we have had one psychiatrist, an optometrist, three medical doctors, a sur-plus of lawyers, one former high ranking member of the FBI, sev-eral technicians of all sorts, a number of teachers, one man who had his own hot dog stand, and a New York city garbage man. Prob-ably what makes us most unique is this mix of people converging from California to Vermont, from North Dakota to Texas, and rang-ing in age from 24 to 69. Throw in the former high school drop-outs and the PhD's, and it all creates an atmosphere of interdepen-dence where everyone seems to be quite comfortable."

> "I've checked into various forms of priesthood. I am told that I need four years of college and four years of semi-nary. I don't have any money to pay for this. Does this mean I'm misinterpreting the call?" Mike Naselli, Florida

"It's fairly safe to say that the cost of seminary education should not be a factor that would stop someone from pursuing the priesthood," notes Father Richard Siepka, Rector of Christ the King Seminary in East Aurora, New York. "On a theology level, almost uniformly, a diocese will pick up the immediate costs. Quite a few have plans so that the person can pay the diocese back. Others don't require that."

Most religious communities and seminaries will expect you to enter debt-free, which means no credit card balances, no student loan payments, no financial obligations. If your financial situation poses problems, it is wise to discuss this openly with the vocation director.

After you have completed the paperwork, the application process continues with a series of personal interviews. "First and foremost, we look for men who have an already existing relationship with Jesus so there is an element of faith that has to be there to begin with," says Monsignor Paul Burkard. "That's one of the strongest criteria. Then we look for men who have leadership ability. We also look for men who have that ability to be comfortable with others and have a certain rapport with people so they can invite others on the faith journey and build that personal relationship into a faith relationship. A psychological problem or difficulty in a person's makeup that looks like it will interfere with ministry would be a disqualifying factor."

In 1993, the American Bishops insisted that seminary administrators incorporate psychological assessment into the admissions policy. This means that most dioceses and religious communities will require that you take several standardized psychological tests and undergo an examination by a psychologist. Some dioceses require two or three appointments — one for testing, one for an interview, and one for follow-up. The psychologist will ask about your faith life, your family background, how you deal with emotional issues, your work, your educational background, your sexual history, and the ways you find meaning in life.

"I was interviewed by the Staff Psychologist and five other members of the faculty and staff. A good interview can be an enjoyable experience for both the interviewer and for the interviewee. I was most impressed by the caliber and demeanor of these people." Roger L. Depue, Cromwell, Connecticut

Sister Kathleen Bryant, RSC, acknowledges that some people may feel uncomfortable about the idea of going to a psychologist. "Most likely you will be asked to tell your story rather than be asked question after question," she explains. "In telling your story many of the questions will be answered. If at any time during the interview you feel uncomfortable about something, tell the psychologist."

You will receive follow-up information from the psychologist and your vocation director. If you've been struggling with painful issues from your childhood or family dysfunction, you may be encouraged to undergo additional counseling.

"My parents both died during my first year in a college seminary. I kept an awful lot of the pain inside me. I think if I had opened up earlier, it wouldn't have been so hard later. I ended up seeing a counselor on a regular basis for a while. What a healing, wonderful experience it is to be able to talk honestly and know that nothing is being held over your head. No one can tell you how to fix your problem, but in the process of talking it through, you end up seeing very clearly at some point what you have to do." Father David LiPuma, Buffalo, New York

Some applicants worry about answering questions related to sexuality.

"Some people might think that you have to be a virgin to become a priest. That would disqualify many who are already priests!!!" Mark Mossa, Grand Coteau, Louisiana

Most communities and dioceses require a sustained period of at least two years of celibacy. Questions about sexual orientation could also arise. Policies on acceptance of gay candidates will vary. Father Tim Reker, Executive Director of the National Conference of Catholic Bishops' Secretariat for Vocations and Priestly Formation, says there are some dioceses and religious communities that will automatically rule out a candidate if they discover he has a homosexual orientation. "I would say in most dioceses, the orientation isn't as much an issue as the person's lifestyle. Whether one is homosexual, heterosexual, or bisexual, they must live a chaste life."

> "I was a vocation director from 1981-1986, and I had to fill out a form for some national survey. The question was: *Would you accept a gay priest?* I wrote down yes on the form and sent it to my Provincial. He questioned me on it. I said, 'Well, as long as they're not practicing. To me, that is the issue.' Actually, we already have gay priests. We've had them for a long time, but we never called them gay, and they didn't refer to themselves as gay." Father Vincent O'Malley, CM, Niagara Falls, New York

"The bottom line is: Can a person, no matter what his sexual orientation, effectively minister to other people?" observes Monsignor Paul Burkard. "Throughout history there have been very effective homosexual and heterosexual priests. Does a homosexual bring some baggage to the priesthood that may prevent him from being a totally effective minister? Some people say that's true. Some say there are issues around homosexuality dealing with belonging and security that may condition how effective he is as a priest. I don't know if there's any research on that to prove it. Does it affect the fraternity of priests? In the past, it was not public knowledge if there was a homosexual priest. There wasn't any open awareness of it and they were treated like everybody else. Are there homophobic priests who would find it difficult to minister with a homosexual priest? Sure. Are there healthy heterosexual priests who would find it uncomfortable? Sure. I think you'll find a range of responses depending on the level of comfort among heterosexual priests and how militant a homosexual priest might be about homosexual issues."

> "My take on it is this: What is your starting point? The starting point for any priest should be the need to proclaim the Good News and to bring God's reign to people. If your starting point is that you are a gay priest, and that becomes your issue, then it colors everything that you do. I say that starting point is wrong and you're going to run into problems. If your starting point is not rooted in the Gospel and in faith, you're going to go astray." Father Kevin Creagh, CM, Niagara Falls, New York

Another sticky question is whether or not someone who is divorced can be considered a candidate for priesthood. The answer is a qualified yes, provided that the person has obtained an ecclesiastical annulment.

> "Following my divorce and annulment, I couldn't understand why I suddenly found God to be so significant in my life. I know that my faith grew during my personal difficulties, that God was not far from me and was supporting me through the pain. I knew that God was holding me up and I knew that he was calling me to service." Father Bob Couto, Nashua, New Hampshire

"We like to deal with those cases on a very personal and individual basis," explains Father Paul Etienne, Vocation Director for the Archdiocese of Indianapolis. "We do not tell divorced men that we won't accept them. But I normally tell them that we need signs that they are exceptional candidates before we would feel comfortable moving ahead with it. We do move into a discernment process with them, but we tell them up front that this is a pretty significant issue, and we need to see some very strong evidence that

they are being called to priesthood in this archdiocese before we
are willing to move ahead with it."

"Part of my application to the seminary was applying to
the small liberal arts college affiliated with the University
of Western Ontario. They are specialized and it is a hard
college to get in. You needed an average much better than
I had. So I didn't get in. I had to go back to high school
and get my average up. I did, and I finally got in. I wasn't
sure I had the brains to do it. That was one of my biggest
worries. But I had the brains. I just wasn't applying myself."
Paul MacNeil, St. Catharine's, Ontario

"By far, the thing that would disqualify most people is their
inability to keep up with the academic program," notes Monsignor
Paul Burkard. "Most rejections are because they haven't proven academically that they can handle this kind of program."

"I'm 32 years old. I know this sounds crazy, but I believe
God is calling me into the priesthood. Why crazy, you may
ask? Well, I am starting RCIA next week. I realize that I
have much to learn about the Church and my relationship
with it. Has anyone had a pair of shoes that just seemed to
fit perfectly and felt good? Well, that is the way I feel about
Catholicism and entering the priesthood." Charles Burt,
Austin, Texas

It's not unusual for converts to Catholicism to show an interest in the priesthood — especially in that initial burst of fervor
which accompanies conversion. Most dioceses will require a two
or three year wait before an application for priesthood is accepted
from a new Catholic. Likewise, fallen-away Catholics, who return
to the faith after being away for a while, are often required to wait
a few years.

At the end of the application process, three things could happen: You will be accepted. You will be told that your application is

being deferred until certain conditions, such as psychological counseling or academic requirements, are met. Or you will be told that you don't meet the qualifications and have not been accepted.

> "I had a bad experience trying to gain entry into the priesthood. I spoke with the Vocation Director for the diocese. I told him of my depressions, my teenage suicide attempts, and the antidepressant drugs that I took in the past. I told him I would be able to empathize more with people as a result. He told me the priesthood had no use for mentally unstable people. I felt crushed. I don't think the Church should discriminate against people's pasts as long as they got their act together. In my opinion, it's people like this who would make excellent priests." N.M., Florida

What many people don't realize is that there are certain impediments outlined in canon law that can exclude someone from admission to a seminary or a religious order. They include suicide attempts, heresy, insanity, psychic disorders, and acts of murder. If you are not accepted because of one of these factors, the vocation director has a responsibility of explaining this to you fully.

> "I think that one of the things that's missing sometimes is the realization that the call to the priesthood is not your choice. This is not your personal right. The call to priesthood is a grace, and it is animated through the ecclesial structure of the Church. The Church calls forth and tries to recognize in certain individuals, 'Yes, there is someone who is priestly.' Therefore, we offer to them the sacrament of ordination. It's not a right. It's a gift of grace." Father Joseph Gatto, Vice Rector, Christ the King Seminary

"What we are essentially saying is that it would be unfair to candidates to ask them to do something that they are not capable of doing," explains Father Robert V. Hotz, SJ. "It is not just to invite a person into what promises to be a frustrating life." Even St. Ignatius of Loyola saw this as a difficult dilemma: "Ignatius desires that the person dismissed should: (1) go forward 'without shame or dishonor'; (2) be sent 'with as much love and charity... and as much consoled in the Lord as possible'; and (3) be given 'direction whereby he may find another good means to serve God,'" Father Hotz explains.

If you still feel called to the priesthood, you are free to apply to another religious order or to establish residence and apply to another diocese.

> "If God wants you as a priest, he's going to keep calling."
> James W.J. Stroud, Henderson, Texas

"But before you begin exploring elsewhere, take some time out to reflect on the experience, to pray for the faith to see the whole picture of your life," advises Sister Kathleen Bryant, RSC. "Go back to the basics of your faith, remembering that God loves you and delights in you. Your baptismal call is your deepest, most profound call."

If another door opens, it may be a sign for you to walk through it. If doors keep closing, it may be a sign that God is not calling you to the priesthood. There have been cases, however, when a closed door opens unexpectedly after a person has given up trying.

> "After I graduated from college, I felt that God was calling me to become a religious order priest. A brain tumor that I had when I was eight years old, left me with some vision problems, and none of the orders I checked into would accept me because I am considered officially disabled. I was 31-years-old, and had given up hope, when a priest at the Immaculata Retreat House said, 'Why don't you try the Oblates?' He put me in touch with the vocation director and I entered their house of formation this year." Bernard LaCasse, Willimantic, Connecticut

Once you are accepted into a religious community or a diocesan formation program, your life will begin to move in different directions. Much of that movement will be dictated by the religious community or the diocese. They will take into consideration your talents, your interests, and your abilities. They may ask your opinion. In the end you will be enrolled in a novitiate, a pre-theology program, or a seminary.

> "My advice is to go for it. It's not going to hurt you to take a year and learn who you are, how to pray, how to study. Make a commitment to stay for a full year. You can't just go with the movements of your own emotion when you are considering a vocation. You really need the staying power of time, of reflection." Father Jim Bastian, Amherst, New York

Chapter Notes

Sister Kathleen Bryant, R.S.C., tells candidates... and f.: Bryant, p. 111.
"Most likely you will be asked to tell your story...": Ibid., pp. 117-118.
...there are certain impediments...: Code of Canon Law, 1983, canons 1040-1049.
"What we are essentially saying is...": Robert V. Hotz, SJ, "Saying No and Letting Go," *Horizon*, Summer, 1992, p. 42.
"Ignatius desires that the person dismissed should...": Ibid., (St. Ignatius Loyola, *Constitutions*, nos. 223-226).
"But before you begin exploring elsewhere...": Bryant, pp. 123-124.

CHAPTER 10

The Path Toward Priesthood

"Once you're in the seminary it's a whole new way of living, a whole new environment. You really get serious about who you are and what your vocation is. You start living it out a little bit." John Polasik, Gowanda, New York

"A seminarian is a man studying for the priesthood. That entails a struggle, but the seminary is a safe place to struggle. It's not a bad struggle. It's a good struggle. I don't wake up every day and think, 'Oh, my God, what am I going to struggle with today?' It's not like that. Some days it is, because our lives are somewhat institutionalized and structured, but it's also a place where if God throws me a curve ball I can rely on the fact that other seminarians can help me through the process without going through it by myself." Paul Salemi, East Aurora, New York

"I would say a seminarian is a man who enters an institution to learn how to minister to God's people. He learns how to heal the psychological and emotional wounds in his own life. He learns whether celibacy is going to be a gift or a cross. He learns how to minister and work with people of other faiths and other cultures. If I had to define who I was, this is how I would do it." Tim Bohen, West Seneca, New York

Paul MacNeil was in his fourth year of the minor seminary in London, Ontario, when he decided to leave. "I left for the exact same reason that I went in," he explains. "It was a response to something inside me. I was 21 years old. The ministry I was doing was extremely difficult, and I had this gnawing feeling that there had to be more to life than this. I remember sitting in the chapel, and saying very clearly to God, 'No, I'm not going to do this. I'm out of here.'"

After leaving, Paul continued to go to school, and ended up with graduate degrees in philosophy. He also continued to pursue challenging ministries, which eventually led him to Calcutta, where he worked as a volunteer bathing the sick, washing clothes, feeding people too weak to feed themselves, and preparing the dead for burial at Prem Dan, one of Mother Teresa's homes for the dying and destitute.

During a visit with Mother Teresa one evening, she asked Paul when he was going into the seminary. "I gave her a blank stare and told her I had been in the seminary for four years," he recalls.

"A vocation is a beautiful gift," Mother Teresa replied. "Don't throw it away that easily."

Three years later, Paul was teaching English to school children in South Korea when he decided it was time to return to the seminary. "Mother Teresa's words were always in the back of my mind and in the back of my heart," he admits.

Paul did not return to the seminary with the attitude that his discernment process was over, however. He realizes that one of the main functions of a seminary is to test whether a candidate really has a vocation.

Father Tim Reker agrees. He tells the story of some surprise visitors one evening, when he was serving as Rector of Immaculate Heart of Mary College Seminary in the Diocese of Winona, Minnesota:

> I was preparing a homily, and in walks this guy with his wife. We had gone to the seminary together, but he left after the first year. He came back to show his wife where

he had gone to school. After a little tour, we sat down in
my office, and he said, "I spent the best year of my life at
IHM Seminary."
"I really appreciate you saying that to me," I told him, "but
if I were married and my wife were sitting next to me, I'm
not sure I would say that!"
We all laughed.

"I tell that story to reassure people who think they might have
a vocation, but aren't sure," Father Reker says. "You've got to check
it out. If you are not being called, you'll find out. It's not like you
just go on and on without ever knowing. The time spent in the seminary or in discernment is time well spent. Even if you find out that
you aren't called, you'll find that you've deepened your relationship
with God and your understanding of yourself. You can go on to
serve the world and the Church in a different way."

In the days before the Second Vatican Council, most young
men entered the seminary with the feeling that they wanted to
become priests, but with a sense of uncertainty as to whether or
not they could make it through the rigors of academics and formation:

"I decided that if I could pass the courses, I'd continue."
Father Gilio Dipre, Erie, Pennsylvania

"The word discernment would never have been spoken in
those pre-Vatican II days," explains Monsignor Paul Burkard. "In
those days the structure did the discerning for you. If the seminary
decided to keep you, you stayed. If they decided you weren't a suit-
able candidate, you left. Internally, there was certainly an element
of discernment going on as your prayer life developed and you saw
what priests do, but it wouldn't have been called discernment."

Today, there is a different emphasis on discerning God's call.
Men are encouraged to test their vocations in several stages that
begin before they enter the seminary and continue right up to the
point of ordination. "That's why seminarians sometimes take off and

work in a department store or in construction for a summer," admits Father Jim Bastian. "They evaluate what happened in the academic year, and they ask themselves, 'Do I want to try this another year? Is there still something there?' Very few guys go to the seminary knowing for sure that they are called to the priesthood. Three guys left the seminary when I was there. Two of them are married now, and I know that they well be great husbands and great fathers."

> "Someone asked me the other day how many guys at the seminary were going to make it. I said, 'It's not a fair question because whether it's one year or six months, something has affected you by being in the seminary. There's no making it or not making it. Ordination is a continuation of the gift God has given us. Even if I were not to be ordained, the experience of the seminary would make me a better Christian and a better person.'" Paul Salemi, East Aurora, New York

The word, seminarian, comes from the Latin word for seed. Like any "seed," seminarians need to be nurtured if they are to grow and bloom. In 1993, the National Conference of Catholic Bishops issued guidelines for a program of formation that would help seminaries prepare candidates for the priesthood. The bishops stressed that the seminary must move the seminarians toward the service of Christ with a deep understanding of Scripture, a sound education in theology, a firm knowledge of Church teachings, a solid foundation in ethics and morality, a comprehensive review of Church history, and meaningful exposure to social justice issues. They will also be trained in homiletics, in how to say Mass, in how to administer the Sacraments, and how to advise and counsel people.

This kind of intense academic formation has a threefold purpose:

- The future priest needs philosophical training to understand and meet the questions and challenges of secular society.
- The future priest needs to know enough not to confuse

morality and religion. He must be able to defend basic moral principles without an appeal to faith.

• The future priest needs a strong foundation in Catholic dogma so nothing will blur the difference between Catholicism and other Christian faiths.

"Such learning will not come easily or automatically," the bishops admitted. "Rather is it the result of effort and hard work. But given the depth and breadth of the theological sciences, nothing less than a thorough education will suffice to supply a sure foundation for fruitful leadership for the years ahead."

> "The best teachers that I had were the ones who inspired an ongoing love for learning. I remember one priest saying, 'You may not know all the answers, but you will be able to know where to go to get the answers.' That was very important because life changes and all sorts of things develop. As a priest, you have no idea what you'll be involved in, such as housing work or hospital work. The seminary develops in you a capacity for learning and the discipline to study the issues. I would tell seminarians to give themselves as much as possible to their studies." Bishop Henry J. Mansell, Diocese of Buffalo

You will also have opportunities for active pastoral ministry. "Academic work and pastoral ministry come to reinforce one another," the bishops wrote. "This mutual interaction also helps a seminarian to sense the presence of God in these experiences and to relate their life in Christ to the service of God's people."

Most dioceses require a year of hands-on parish experience before ordination. Some seminarians will be offered pastoral internships or summer assignments in parishes or other ministries. These kinds of experiences give seminarians first hand opportunities to work in youth ministry, social justice, rural ministry, ecumenism, care of the sick, elderly and dying, religious education and evangelization. They meet different types of people in a variety of cultural and ethnic settings:

"My ministry last year was teaching classes for the RCIA. This year I'm involved in something called Small Christian Communities. Every other Thursday after Mass at 7:30 p.m., people who want to be part of the group stay. I read a short meditation. Then I let them sit with that for 15 minutes or so of silent prayer. After that I give a 15 minute teaching. After the teaching, we break up into small groups of five or six people each. We just talk. Most of the talk is about the teaching or the meditation but it doesn't have to be. It's designed to get people in the parish to get to know each other and see familiar faces when they come to Mass." John Fletcher, Ottawa, Ontario

In some dioceses, candidates for the priesthood will spend a year in a parish as transitional deacons:

"As a deacon, I was sent to my home parish. I was treated like a priest. I had my days on duty. I did all the baptisms. I preached at every Mass on Sunday. When I preached I'd tell the people about God's love. They responded to that. It was a very positive experience." Monsignor John Madsen, Depew, New York

"The seminary is a school of human virtue, of growth in honesty, integrity, intellectual rigor, hard work, tolerance, and discipline, leavened by humor and healthy enjoyment," the American bishops noted. "The seminary must also be a school of spiritual growth in which seminarians are formed into men of prayer, imbued with those virtues that only grace can bring: faith, hope and charity."

Daily Mass and the Liturgy of the Hours form the foundation of seminary prayer life, but candidates are also taught the necessity of sustained personal prayer.

The late Joseph Cardinal Bernardin did not come to a full understanding of the importance of prayer in his priesthood until after he became Archbishop of Cincinnati. During dinner one evening with three young priests — two of whom he had recently ordained — he admitted that he was finding it difficult to pray. He asked the priests if they could help him.

The three priests responded with two questions: "Are you sincere in what you request?" and "Do you really want to turn this around?"

"What could I say?" he later recalled. "I couldn't say no after what I had just told them!"

The priests' advice was simple. They told him that he had to adopt the spirituality and follow the practices that he so often told other priests to follow.

Years later, Cardinal Bernardin recalled that this was a turning point in his life:

> These priests helped me understand that you have to give what they called, and what many spiritual directors today call, "quality time" to prayer. It can't be done "on the run." You have to put aside good time, quality time. After all, if we believe that the Lord Jesus is the Son of God, then of all persons to whom we give of ourselves, we should give him the best we have.

Father Bob Bedard agrees. In 1975, after twenty years as a priest, he underwent what he calls "a turning point."

> I was at a Life in the Spirit Seminar. The leaders were talking about the First Corinthian gifts: miracles, tongues, prophecy, discernment of spirits, and so on. They urged us to ask specifically for some of these gifts. I am not the kind of person that ordinarily would get involved in the external manifestation of holding hands in the air and things like that. In fact, I am quite the opposite. So I was saying to the Lord, "If you don't want to give me any of those gifts, that's okay. What I do need desperately, however, is the gift of prayer."
> My prayer had gone down the tubes. I think it was because I had gotten into the heresy of works. I was very busy. My individual response to the Lord got lost in the idea that my

work was my prayer — which it isn't, of course. Work is work. Prayer is prayer. You can offer work to the Lord, but it's not prayer. So I said, "I don't even know if there is such a thing as a gift of prayer, but if there is, I want it." I re-dedicated my life to Jesus Christ, and I asked for the full-ness of the Holy Spirit, which I had never done before. Within a day, I had the gift of prayer. It was absolutely un-mistakable. I had a desire to pray that I had never experi-enced before, and I had a capacity to pray that I had never experienced before. Within a few weeks, I was praying a hour a day. I had changed from being a night person, who never went to bed before midnight, to being a morning person, who was up every morning at quarter to six for an hour of prayer before the day started — and I loved it! I still do, and I would never give it up. It was a real gift. It turned my life around.

In their formation guidelines, the American bishops noted that: "In the solitude of their own prayer, priests encounter in a special and personal way the Lord whom they proclaim and cel-ebrate in public ministry. In personal prayer, priests find the strength, the courage and the grace to live an authentic priestly life. They hear God's continuing call as their lives unfold in active min-istry and they remember that it is God alone who 'gives the growth.'"

"A good prayer life will sustain you through the difficul-ties. Prayer has to be the foundation because we could not do any of this if we were doing it ourselves. Prayer gave me the strength and the grace to get through the academ-ics in the seminary and be where I am today." Father Rob-ert Wozniak, Buffalo, New York

Most seminarians also meet with their spiritual director at least once a month. "Spiritual direction represents a relationship in the internal forum which enjoys confidentiality," the bishops explain. "Seminarians should avail themselves of this unique opportunity for growth by being as honest and transparent as possible with their spiritual directors."

A spiritual director will not only introduce you to different forms of prayer, he will also help you to integrate your prayer life into everything you do.

> "My spiritual director helped me set priorities and balance my time between studying, prayer, ministry, and outside interests. That's a key thing: to get away and do something that relaxes you. I enjoyed walking. On the mornings when I walked, I knew that nothing would happen that I couldn't handle. When I didn't walk, I could tell the difference. It's easy to get overwhelmed by everything that's going on. You have to be able to step away and relax." Father David LiPuma, Buffalo, New York

Another important aspect of seminary life is community. Father Piero Coda, Professor of Dogmatic Theology at the Pontifical Lateran University, notes that in the past seminarians struggled with the question: "Who am I?" "Today the emphasis is different," he says, "and the question is: 'Who are we?' And that question leads to another: 'Where are we going?'"

The American bishops emphasized that community life in the seminary plays an essential role in the development of future priests. "The give-and-take between those who share the same vocational goal provides mutual support and promotes increased tolerance while allowing fraternal connection to take place," the bishops wrote. "Community life affords the opportunity for the development of leadership skills and individual talents. It can also motivate seminarians to develop a sense of self-sacrifice and a spirit of collaboration. The seminarians and the faculty form the center of the seminary community. This center needs careful cultivation so that the distinctive aims of seminary formation can be achieved."

Father Richard Siepka, Rector of Christ the King Seminary, agrees: "With more priests living alone in rectories, what I hope the seminary does is create a need for community among priests and seminarians who share a unique role of service in the Church. The time in the seminary should create the recognition that we need each other in the priesthood."

"Some of the best spiritual direction is done by one seminarian to another. It's more personal. They open their hearts
to each other. Some of the sessions I had in the seminary
were as good as any that I had with a spiritual director. With
another seminarian you know that you're both in the same
boat." Father John Mergenhagen, Derby, New York

The common thread that runs through all these aspects of
seminary life is priestly formation. Seminarians are usually assigned
a formation director. The goal of formation is to establish priestly
attitudes and personal habits that will continue after ordination. The
formation director will help you examine your attitudes about sexuality, morality, ethics. He will pose the questions: What is a priest?
Who is a priest in relation to the community of believers? Can you
conform to that image of priesthood?

"The focus of formation is to help you recognize within yourself a priestly identity," explains Father Joseph Gatto, Vice Rector
of Christ the King Seminary. "The seminary can't give you a priestly
identity. The seminary can offer you styles of prayer, spiritual direction, retreats, classes, academics, and a lot of other things, but
you have to take advantage of that and work hard. It's discipline.
It's not something that is given to you as a gift. True gifts are something earned. You have to work hard and you have to commit yourself to them."

Father Raymond Hostie, SJ, agrees: "The years of formation
give candidates a chance to realize their talents and gifts and show
their capacities, and this means that certain difficulties are inevi-
table and even necessary if real growth is to be assured."

Seminarians go through regular evaluations with their formation director. The director looks at maturity, self-awareness, spiritual life, good judgment, capacity for leadership, a desire to work
collaboratively with others, professional manners, and the ability
to maintain friendships.

"I remember formation as an opportunity to really grow in
some areas. There were times that I wanted to just throw

my hands up in total disgust and say, 'All right, I will just move out of here.' After my second year I came pretty close to that. I got a really bad evaluation from my formation director. It wasn't until a year or two later that I realized that of the ten things he said, three or four were right on the money. I really did have to grow in those areas. The other six I thought were unreasonable and totally untrue, but it wasn't bad that I thought about those, either. That is the hard work of formation. We are challenged to look at our lives and to really consider the areas where we need to grow. It was definitely a time of great challenge and great personal growth." Father Ted Jost, Tonawanda, New York

Once a year, a written evaluation is sent to the bishop or the superior of the religious order. As ordination approaches, a probation period may be recommended for candidates who do not meet the qualification or still struggle with doubts.

"It's very hard for any seminary to prepare a man for priesthood," admits Father Joseph Gatto. "You can talk about the experience of sitting in a confessional, but no one can really prepare you for the first time you hear a confession or the first time you find yourself in a hospital with a family who is crying because their father is dying. What a seminary needs to do is place an individual in relationship to the Lord and to the Church. Then, when the Sacrament of Ordination occurs, the things you learned and the grace of the sacrament will sustain you."

Some priests will tell you that they loved their seminary training:

"They were the best and most enjoyable years of my life. I deepened my commitment to the Lord. My vision of the priesthood and my understanding of the Church developed. I got to know people from all over the East Coast. I made lifelong friends. I experienced community life for the first time. The instructors were strong theologically and emphasized the need to know doctrine. They showed us how to teach and preach in a way that people would understand. They emphasized the importance of maintaining a spiritual life because a priest is above all a man of prayer. They taught us to make time for prayer every day because prayer fuels one's ministry. They taught us how to deal with people. They prepared us for the nitty-gritty of pastoral life." Father Don Guglielmi, East Haven, Connecticut

Most priests will tell you that the seminary had good points and bad:

"I think the seminary prepared me very well academically. I have a good grounding and good theological constructs. I have a good sense of what the Church is and what the Church must provide for people. I have been given a good prayer life. I would say my formation was good. Things that I felt went overboard involved the psycho-babble. It's almost like being in a fish bowl. From the day you say you want to be a priest, they start watching you." Father Kevin Creagh, CM, Niagara Falls, New York

Today's seminaries are cautious for a reason. With the explosion of sexual scandals among clergy in the 1980's, a whole new attitude has developed in terms of making sure that a seminarian has a sufficient degree of psychological and sexual maturity. In *Pastores Dabo Vobis*, Pope John Paul II urged seminaries to prepare each candidate for celibacy "so that he may know, appreciate, love and live celibacy according to its true nature and according to its real purposes, that is, for evangelical, spiritual and pastoral motives."

Chaste celibacy is often referred to as a "gift." In the next chapter, we'll take a closer look at the gift of celibacy and how priests incorporate that gift into their lives.

Chapter Notes

"I gave her a blank stare..." and f.: Dave Condren, "Area seminarian recalls inspiration he received from Mother Teresa," *Buffalo News*, September 13, 1997.

This kind of intense academic formation has a threefold purpose...: Jude P. Dougherty, "Academic

Component of Priestly Formation," *Analecta*, Vol. II, Cromwell, Connecticut: Holy Apostles College and Seminary, 1988.

"Such learning will not come easily...": *Program of Priestly Formation*, [337], p. 64.

"Academic work and pastoral ministry come to reinforce one another...": *Program of Priestly Formation*, [402], p. 75.

"The seminary is a school of human virtue...": *Program of Priestly Formation*, [296], p. 52.

The late Joseph Cardinal Bernardin..." and f.: Joseph Cardinal Bernardin, *The Gift of Peace*, Chicago: Loyola Press, 1997, pp. 5-6.

"In the solitude of their own prayer...": *Program of Priestly Formation*, [76], p. 20.

"Spiritual direction represents a relationship...": *Ibid.*, [281], p. 55.

"Today the emphasis is different...": Piero Coda, "A Spirituality for Today," *Priests of the Future: Formation and Communion*, Rev. Michael Mulvey, ed., New York: New City Press, 1991, p. 22.

"The give-and-take between those who share...": *Program of Priestly Formation*, [304], pp. 59-60.

"The years of formation give candidates...": Hostie, p. 134.

"so that he may know, appreciate, love and live celibacy...": Pope John Paul II, *Pastores Dabo Vobis*, [50].

CHAPTER 11

The Gift of Celibacy

"In a homily one day, the pastor of my parish talked about celibacy. He said celibacy is not all that bad. When people ask him, 'Don't you feel bad that you don't have a family?' He says, 'Not at all. Every child that I baptize becomes my child, and through the years as that child grows up, I am raising that child in the Church.' He said there is not one night that goes by that he is not invited to people's homes for dinner. He said that people love their priests and they make priests part of their family." Michael Barone, Kenmore, New York

"I feel attracted to the priesthood but I don't know if it is God's will and I don't know if I can be chaste." Daniel M. Bettendorf, Grand Coteau, Louisiana

"The first thing my friends would say if they knew I was thinking about the priesthood is, 'You know you can't have sex. You can't get married. Are you dumb? Or are you gay?' My brother says he would be a priest in a second if he could get married. I haven't decided." Michael Buscaglia, Amherst, New York

There's a joke about a young priest answering the door at the rectory and finding a beautiful, young woman standing there. His sexual interests were instantly aroused, but he managed to take care of her questions in a calm and professional manner.

Afterward, he went to the pastor and said, "I don't think I can do this again. The next time she comes to the door, could you handle it?"

"Sure," the pastor replied. "These things are no problem after you reach age 70."

The next time the woman rang the bell, the pastor answered the door. Afterward, he came back to the young priest and said, "I think the age is 80!"

The issue of celibacy is one of the most difficult challenges faced by a man discerning a vocation to the priesthood today. "Celibacy is a struggle," admits Father Paul Golden, CM. "I don't know of any man who can say, 'This is absolutely not an issue for me.' The choice of celibacy may be clear and easy for this year or even for several years, but it will not be easy at other times."

Bishop Paul Loverde agrees. "We need straight talk about celibacy," he says. "That's a necessity for young people today. We live in a world surrounded by sexual explosions. We are bombarded. I think we need to tell young people what it means to live celibately. We have to be very straight and clear about that."

In their guidelines on Priestly Formation, the American bishops define celibacy as one of the most fundamental responses to Jesus' call to radical discipleship for the sake of the kingdom. "The ideal of a celibate, single life is based on Scripture (Mt 19:12 and 1 Cor 7:7ff., and 36-38). Living without a wife and family as Jesus did is a powerful witness in the world, which creates a heightened relationship between the priest and the people. This radical commitment makes a priest more focused in his ministry."

To be celibate does not mean that you must live in emotional isolation. It does not mean that you will be miserable and lonely. "Certainly Jesus was no gloomy celibate," suggests Father Thomas P. Rausch, SJ, professor and chair of theological studies at Loyola Marymount University in Los Angeles. "Jesus was good company. His celibacy did not cut him off from other people, but made him more available to them. The stories in the Gospels showing that people felt free to approach him suggest that he was warm and affectionate with them."

"Sometimes priests get into this thing, 'Look at me. I have this celibacy thing on me.' Well, I know some married people that struggle every day much more than I do. We all struggle and we all need God's grace. That's the bottom line." Father Kevin Creagh, CM, Niagara Falls, New York

In every person's life — whether they are young or old, rich or poor, married or single — there is a deep, existential loneliness. "This loneliness is the call from within because our hearts are restless until they rest in God," says Bishop Loverde. "God is the only one who can ultimately satisfy our deepest longings. In my 33 years as a priest, there have been times of loneliness, but the more I am open to the Lord Jesus, the more I see him as my significant other. When I allow Jesus to be present to me and to deepen that relationship, those moments of loneliness are absorbed. The Lord made us with a longing to be with another. That's very human. The Lord would not call me to be a priest to frustrate the longing that he put in me. For a priest, the bond with a unique other is with the Lord Jesus. If a priest doesn't have a relationship with the Lord Jesus then there's going to be someone or something else in his life. I think we need straight talk about that. We have to put those things out very clearly."

"Sometimes, it's difficult, especially when you have a nice friendship with a woman and you know that sex would just naturally flow out of this relationship. But you don't do it. You go home and sit there frustrated. At times like that, I say to God, 'All right. I didn't do it. Now there's this empty space inside of me. What are you going to put in this space?' What comes is a tremendous peace and a tremendous closeness to God — not all the time — but very often. That might be because I pray with an expectation and I know why I'm celibate. I think everyone has to come up with their own reason." Monsignor John Madsen, Depew, New York

In *A Delicate Dance: Sexuality, Celibacy and Relationships Among Catholic Clergy and Religious*, Sheila Murphy identified four reasons that priests and religious frequently cite for celibacy. They include: "spouse of Christ," "availability for ministry," "countercultural witness" and what she calls "the oft-repeated lament of many diocesan clerics, 'Because I have to as a requirement of being a priest today!'"

"I have found through my research and workshop contacts that all four definitions remain active among today's vowed celibates," she notes, "but the most commonly endorsed of all is 'availability for ministry.' Some report that they shift from definition to definition, depending upon where they are developmentally, both spiritually and psychologically."

For many, celibacy is seen as a sacrifice. "One of the things I've always said is that celibacy has to be based on the fact that what you are giving up is something good," says Father Richard Siepka, Rector of Christ the King Seminary. "Celibacy is not a holier way of living. It's a different way of living. It confirms the sacredness of marriage. Marriage is a sacrament. Marriage is based on God's plan for the world. Marriage is such a good that the demand for a priest to sacrifice something so beautiful for the sake of God's people makes celibacy that much more powerful."

"Many feel that simply because the idea of marriage or fathering children is attractive to them, they couldn't possibly be a priest. Wouldn't it be awful if we only had priests who felt disdain for marriage and didn't like kids! Rather, one should choose to become a priest out of a conviction that life as a priest will best achieve God's will and best make use of the gifts and talents which God has given you." Mark Mossa, Grand Coteau, Louisiana

Some say celibacy itself is a gift. "Celibacy that is God-given and sustained is a gift that enriches the life of the person who is called to it," says Bishop Matthew H. Clark of Rochester, New York.

> "I don't feel that I am a natural celibate. Whether it is ge-
> netics, erogenous zones, or hormones, or whatever, I knew
> that celibacy would be a tremendous struggle for me. It
> goes against every natural inclination I have as a young
> person with normal sexual urges. But unlike our culture
> which says, 'Sex is cool. Act on it,' the Church says, 'Sex is
> cool. God gave you those urges, but you're not an animal.
> You don't have to act on it.' God makes celibate priesthood
> possible because of his love for his people. God is the one
> who makes it possible for a healthy young guy like me to
> give up sex for the sake of the kingdom. That's awe-inspir-
> ing." Father Ted Jost, Tonawanda, New York

In a recent survey, some seminarians described celibacy as a discipline, which is best developed by practicing it daily. "As anyone who has a talent must stay in condition to keep that talent healthy and growing, so too, do some seminarians espouse this approach to celibacy," the study concluded.

The best place to develop the discipline of celibacy is in a seminary or a house of formation. "Seminarians must judge if they themselves have the gift of celibacy and before ordination give assurance to the Church that they can live the permanent commitment to celibacy with authenticity and integrity," the American bishops explained in their guidelines to priestly formation.

When seminarians were asked what best helps them prepare for a life of celibacy, most mentioned prayer: "Being in touch with Jesus"; "Creating a loving relationship with God"; "Building a personal, special relationship with the person of Jesus"; "Linking up understanding and enlightenment with celibacy"; "A daily offering to God"; "Staying in touch with a sense of God's call"; "The means of becoming Christ centered"; "A conduit of grace."

Some of the seminarians linked prayer with other factors: "Having a good confidant"; "Utilizing spiritual direction"; "Speaking about celibacy openly"; "Studying and discussing it."

"It is not the case that I no longer have desires or feelings about women. I do. These desires are not easy to dismiss, either. However, this is something that I don't do by myself. I supply the will, the decision, and God supplies the grace to accomplish this. It isn't finished once and for all at the time of making the decision. These are feelings that come and go, and will probably come and go for the rest of my life." John Fletcher, Ottawa, Ontario

One of the difficulties faced by men discerning priesthood today is the awareness that celibacy was not a law made by Jesus or by the apostles. They know that while a tradition of celibacy has been present since the earliest days of the Church, there was also a tradition in the early Church of a married clergy. This tradition continued in the Eastern Rites, where priests are still allowed to marry before ordination, but bishops must remain celibate. Today, the Church also allows married Protestant ministers, who convert to Catholicism, to be ordained as married Catholic priests. It's not unreasonable for some men discerning priesthood to wonder: *Why should I live out my life as a celibate when in a few years or a few decades, this law might be changed?* The reality, however, is that you could wait an entire lifetime for the laws to change. You have to ask yourself: *Am I willing to take that gamble? What does God want me to do? What do I really want to do?*

"When I think of my calling I disregard those issues because I don't believe my calling is coming from me. I believe it's coming from God. A lot of times I wish I didn't have the calling. Sometimes I wish God would one day open up a door and say, 'Forget that idea, Ray. I want you to get married.' I think I would jump up and down and say, 'All right!' It's very difficult to give yourself totally to God." Raymond Barrett, Rochester, New York

Another difficult issue related to celibacy is the subject of sexual orientation. "To conclude, 'I don't need to worry about sexual orientation because I'm celibate,'" suggests Sheila Murphy, "is to beg the question and to live a lie since our ability to be comfortable with others' orientation is dependent upon our ability to be comfortable with our own. This does not mean that we necessarily have to proclaim our orientation to the entire world to be 'real'; that could be meaningless and counterproductive to many ministers and those to whom they minister. It does demand a personal honesty, however, which we may or may not choose to share with others."

Father Thomas P. Rausch, SJ, urges every priest and seminarian, whether heterosexual or homosexual, to address his own fears and prejudices:

> Too often one still hears the put-downs of gay people and dismissive jokes which come under the expression "gay bashing." These should not be tolerated among priests.
>
> At the same time, there is often a cliquishness among self-identified gay priests, along with ill-concealed contempt for "straights" who are dismissed as insensitive, uncreative, and uninteresting. This kind of reverse stereotyping can be described as heterophobia and is equally offensive.
>
> It is important for each of us to recognize and be comfortable with our sexual identity. But sexual orientation is part of our total identity; it is not or should not be that which defines us. For priests especially to redefine themselves on the basis of sexual orientation is needlessly divisive and usually not helpful to the individual.
>
> A man who defines himself in terms of sexual orientation usually ends up focusing all his energy along those lines. There are many splendid priests who are gay. But a priest who defines himself as a gay priest, rather than as a priest who is also gay, often spends inordinate amounts of time seeking out gay friends, pursuing gay interests, even taking part in gay activities. It is not at all clear that adopting elements of gay lifestyle or going to gay bars is appropriate behavior for a priest committed to celibacy. The same cautions of course would apply to a heterosexual priest who defined himself and structured his activity primarily in terms of his sexual interests.
>
> For priests committed to a celibate life, their personal iden-

tity should be rooted in their priesthood, not in their sexual orientation. To identify themselves and each other as straight or gay priests is to focus on an issue which is not central to their vocation and may indeed distract one from it. Priests are called, like Jesus, to identify with all God's people, not just with those who are like themselves.

Sometimes, a person will mistake the need for intimacy with a need for sex. "Intimacy means the capacity for emotional, physical, and spiritual connectedness with another person," explains Sister Kathleen Bryant, RSC. "Intimacy is not a needy, smothering relationship. Intimacy is the capacity to be truly yourself with another person as well as to create a trust in which the other person can reveal the self as well."

You can find this kind of intimacy in good personal relationships. Some priests find this kind of intimacy with family members. Some find intimacy in the fraternity of priests. Some find it with lay people. Some enter into deeply personal, celibate relationships with a person they find physically and emotionally attractive.

"To gauge how chaste we are, a good practical guideline is the depth and quality of our friendship," says Father Wilke Au, SJ. "To remain at a safe distance from others is not a sign of chastity. On the contrary, it is a kind of unchastity if it prevents us from involving ourselves deeply and caringly in others' lives."

Throughout the history of the Church, beginning with Jesus, Martha and Mary, there are powerful examples of celibate relationships between religious men and women. They include Patrick and Brigid, Francis of Assisi and Clare, John of the Cross and Teresa of Avila, Jane de Chantal and Francis de Sales, Vincent de Paul and Louise de Marillac, Rose of Lima and Martin de Porres.

"Friends share life: visions and values, interests and activities, thoughts and feelings," says Father Vincent O'Malley, CM. "Friends may pass the whole day together and then go home and write or telephone each other to talk about the delight of having been together. They confide in each other what is most private and personal. Because they share deeply, they influence each other deeply."

In *Grace Under Pressure*, a study of effective priests ordained ten to thirty years, several priests talked about their close friendships with women. They admitted that celibacy can be difficult, but not impossible, and the value of the friendship makes it worth the effort:

> "I have one friend in particular with whom I am very close. My celibacy means a lot to her. It means a lot to me. And she is married, has a number of children. But it's a life-giving relationship and without it I wouldn't be the priest that I am."

Father John Mergenhagen, a retreat master at the St. Columban Center in Derby, New York, believes a true understanding of celibacy will come from the East. "The West is so rooted in negative attitudes toward body and sexuality that it will take a long time for us to purify that," he says. "We're so busy discovering the goodness of sex that the next stage might be discovering that there is value in refraining from sex. In the East, many of the non-Christian religions, such as Buddhism, have a deep reverence for celibacy. They have intensive retreats of deep silence, and the participants are asked to refrain from any kind of sexual practice while they are on the retreat. So maybe a deeper understanding of celibacy will come with more dialogue between the East and the West."

Retired Bishop Francis A. Quinn of Sacramento, California offered the following advice to newly ordained priests in Tucson, Arizona:

> Celibacy is not something we possess for once and for all. We are constantly becoming celibate. Because of our upbringing, because of possible unenlightened sexual repression in early years, because of the original clouding of intellect and the weakening of will, because of the need for intimacy, and because of the downright pleasure of genitality, you will find celibacy an unremitting challenge. The following is old-fashioned advice, but there is no other

magic formula. Stay away from the occasions of sin — the persons and places that entice to sin. Calmly understand the nature of sex. Do not be frightened by your sexuality or obsessed with it. Present yourself to the laity as compassionate fellow strugglers, just as the laity are, to live up to Christian sexual ideals. God's way of loving is the only licensed teacher of human sexuality. God's passion created our passion. If we are afraid of our sexuality, we are afraid of God.

While celibacy is always a major concern of men discerning a vocation to the priesthood, many priests would suggest that there is one other promise for diocesan priests and two more for priests in religious communities that are equally important and challenging.

"I think a lot of us would tell you that obedience is ultimately the most difficult." Father Paul Golden, CM, Niagara University

Chapter Notes

"The ideal of a celibate, single life...": Program of Priestly Formation, [64], p. 17.

"Certainly Jesus was no gloomy celibate...": Thomas P. Rausch, SJ, Priesthood Today: An Appraisal, New York: Paulist Press, 1992, p. 59.

Sheila Murphy identified four reasons... and f.: Sheila Murphy, A Delicate Dance: Sexuality, Celibacy and Relationships Among Catholic Clergy and Religious, New York: Crossroad, 1992, p. 65.

"Celibacy that is God-given...": Matthew H. Clark, DD, "The Priesthood and Celibacy," Being a Priest Today. Edited by Donald J. Goergen, Collegeville, Minnesota: Michael Glazier Books, The Liturgical Press, 1992, p. 164.

"As anyone who has a talent...": Seminarians in the Nineties, A National Study of Seminarians in Theology, p. 41.

"Seminarians must judge if they themselves have the gift of celibacy...": Program of Priestly Formation, [292], p. 57.

When seminarians were asked... and f.: Seminarians in the Nineties, A National Study of Seminarians in Theology, p. 41.

"To conclude, 'I don't need to worry about sexual orientation...": Murphy, p. 115.

"Too often one still hears the put-downs...": Rausch, pp. 71-72.

"Intimacy means the capacity...": Bryant, p. 74.

"To gauge how chaste we are...": Wilke Au, SJ, *By Way of the Heart*, New York: Paulist Press, 1989, p. 150.

"Friends share life: visions and values...": Vincent J. O'Malley, CM, *Saintly Companions*, New York: Alba House, 1995, p. 133.

"I have one friend in particular...": James Walsh, and others, *Grace Under Pressure: What Gives Life to American Priests*, Washington, DC: National Catholic Educational Association, 1995, p. 40.

"Celibacy is not something we possess...": Arthur Jones, "At ordination, talk of shared ministry," *National Catholic Reporter*, September 12, 1997.

CHAPTER 12

The Other Two Vows ✝

"For myself, and I think many young Americans, the vow of obedience is a tough one to swallow. Surely, one of the problems is that the priestly vows are almost always seen in a negative rather than a positive light." Mark Mossa, Grand Coteau, Louisiana

"My parents think I would not make a very good priest because I enjoy having things and living in a rich suburb." Brett McLaughlin, Pittsford, New York

"If you are serious about doing God's will and not your own, poverty and obedience will be a great grace — although sometimes painful. Start by simplifying your lifestyle, your prayer style, your expectations, your efforts." Father Michael Dodd, OCD, Brighton, Massachusetts

When other professors at Canisius College start negotiating for salary raises, Father Benjamin Fiore, SJ, doesn't even give it a second thought. "I just sign the contract and send it in," he says. "I never see the money anyway!"

As a Jesuit, Father Fiore took a vow of poverty, which means that except for books, clothes and other incidentals, he owns nothing. Any money he earns goes directly to the Jesuit community.

"It's very freeing," he says. "I've never had to worry about food or shelter. I didn't have to worry about money for my education or money for travel. I did have to ask permission, but once it was approved, I had no worries at all."

The reason Father Fiore has to ask permission for travel or to spend money is that he also took a vow of obedience.

"Obedience plays very strongly in the life of a Jesuit," he explains. "We go where the superior sends us. If we ask to go somewhere and he tells us no, we don't go. The superior always listens to you and to what your needs and desires are. He usually won't put you somewhere that you won't fit. He won't ask you to do things that you can't do. You have a sense that what you are doing is what you ought to do. It removes that question: 'Is this the best thing I can do with my life?' I already know if it's approved, it's good. No problem. Go ahead."

Obedience is a basic component in the lives of both order priests and diocesan priests.

While an order priest promises obedience to his religious superior, a diocesan priest promises obedience to his bishop.

There's an old joke about a bishop, who asked a rebellious young cleric, "Father, don't you recall your ordination day when you put your hands in mine and you pledged obedience to me *or* my successors?"

"Yes, Bishop," the priest said. "I remember."

"Then, why do you disobey me?" the bishop exclaimed.

"I thought it was a multiple choice question," the priest replied.

What really happens on the day of ordination is that a priest promises to obey the bishop *and* his successors.

In an essay intended to help priests and seminarians understand the vows they take, Archbishop Daniel Buechlein, OSB, Father Robert Leavitt, SS, and Father Howard P. Bleichner, SS, explained that this promise "is never made to a bishop or religious superior personally but rather to the office and ministry it serves."

Father Tim Reker, Director of the National Conference of Catholic Bishops' Secretariat on Vocations and Priestly Formation, explains that a bishop has to keep in mind the welfare of the entire diocese. "So we are sometimes asked to do things that we don't particularly care to do. When I was first ordained I had absolutely no say in where I was going. That happened in my second assignment, too. When I was asked to be a chaplain at a college, they checked with me to see if I'd be interested. When my bishop asked me to take the position of rector at Immaculate Heart of Mary College Seminary, he said, 'Unless you have a good reason to say no, I expect you to say yes.' The bishop looked at the responsibility of the assignment, he knew what priests he had available, and he felt that I was the right person at that time for the position. Well, I may have a good reason why this appointment should not happen, and he would take that into consideration. But ultimately the bishop can say, 'Hey, this is where you're going and I don't care!'"

> "Since I have a good bishop it's easy to obey. I accept the direction of the bishop as God's will, rather than try to do my own thing. The virtue of obedience is hard if one is proud or quick to judge." Father Chris Heath, Tustin, California

Father Paul Golden, CM, agrees. "Pride is a deeply rooted experience. To conform my will to God's will and to conform my will to the expression of my superiors, who are portraying God's will, can be very, very difficult."

Part of the difficulty with obedience is that it goes against the grain of what the world teaches. People don't like to be told what to do. Bad experiences with harsh, authoritarian leaders add to lack of trust and lack of respect for authority.

Before the Second Vatican Council, many religious orders took obedience very literally. Superiors were much stricter in terms of requiring permissions for almost everything. Both order priests and diocesan priests could be moved to a new assignment on a moment's notice without any input. It was blind obedience that was sometimes abused by authority figures.

The Second Vatican Council introduced the concept of collegiality, which allows for more give and take in dioceses and in religious communities.

"Now, in most congregations, you don't have to ask permission for everything," explains Father Albert Dilanni, SM. "You can just let the superior know what's going on. He can always say no, but in general, it is a much more adult relationship. Today, most superiors of religious orders are trained to dialogue."

In most dioceses, priest personnel boards assist the bishop in making sure that clergy assignments meet the needs of the priest and the parish. However, the bishop or religious superior retains the right to override the system and act from a position of authority. When that happens, priests are required to obey.

> "I have to say it isn't always easy. There have been times when I have been asked to do something, and I've said, 'I don't think I can do that.' But they've said, 'Yes, you can,' and it has always worked out. I have never said that I definitely would not do something. I can't imagine myself saying that." Father David LiPuma, Buffalo, New York

A certain level of obedience is also expected in the seminary. "No matter how much we might try to form community, the fact is there are people in charge of your formation," explains Father Richard Siepka, Rector of Christ the King Seminary. "The seminarians have to understand that this person has some authority. That does not mean you must follow the formation director blindly because he is the boss. You follow because this person has something of value to offer. It means listening thoroughly to what is being said and trying to understand. It means embracing the rules and not following them grudgingly."

> "For me, obedience was, and still is, the most difficult of the vows we take. We have to be obedient to the authorities, but we also must be obedient to the faith, not only as we see it, but as it is seen and taught and understood by the Church. We have to realize that through our obedience we show others in the Church what it means to be a

man of the Church. We have to realize that obedience is demanded of us for our own good as well as the good of the people we serve." Father Paul Bombadier, Ware, Massachusetts

"To be a follower of Christ is sacrificial," says Father Joseph Gatto. "It begins with obedience to the Gospel. I make that commitment to obedience because I believe the Gospel animates me as a person. It fulfills me as a person. I am going to be obediently sacrificial in giving myself, and sometimes supplanting my personal needs, for the sake of the Gospel."

In the Gospel, there is only one way to follow Jesus authentically and that is the way of the Cross: "If a man wishes to come after me, he must deny his very self, take up his cross, and follow in my steps. Whoever would preserve his life will lose it, but whoever loses his life for my sake and the Gospel's will preserve it" (Mk 8:34-35).

Priests deny themselves many things in order to be of service to the people. Living a life of obedience is part of that denial. Living a life of chaste celibacy is also part of that denial. When you bring together all the things that a priest denies himself, you touch on the mystery of poverty.

Religious order priests take a vow of poverty. Some communities take that vow of poverty very literally and their members deny themselves comforts that most people today consider necessities. For most religious orders, however, the vow of poverty does not necessarily mean that they will actually live in a state of physical deprivation.

"No one says, 'You're only going to have a room with a bed and a bureau.' Those days are over. In some ways, that kind of rigidity made poverty easier. Someone made the decision for you and checked up on you. But now, we have to live poverty in our hearts. We have to ask ourselves, 'Hey, do I really need this?' It comes down to your own personal responsibility for living out the Gospel. That's a little harder." Father Kevin Creagh, CM, Niagara Falls, New York

Today, many religious orders, while not denying the need to practice a certain degree of real material poverty, focus on the importance of spiritual poverty which implies an inner surrender of all that you are, all that you have, and all that you do. "Poverty or simplicity of life is a commitment to a sharing, not only of possessions, but of your time, talent, and presence," explains Sister Kathleen Bryant. "Poverty challenges religious to live simply in joyful dependence on God, standing in solidarity with the poor and challenging the structures that oppress."

Diocesan priests do not take a vow of poverty, but they are called to a life of simplicity.

"Simplicity of life helps us as priests to live more effectively the priesthood of Jesus Christ," explains Father Dennis Schmitz of Kansas City, Kansas. "I don't always model Jesus the Master very well. I get caught between the consumer mentality and the Gospel mentality. We all could live with less and be more fulfilled."

"Some priests have the tendency to take on the lifestyle of a bachelor — owning the finest of clothes, dining in the finest of restaurants, having the most expensive hobbies. This is a scandal. Too much ease and comfort leads to selfishness, pride and a loss of spirituality." Father Chris Heath, Tustin, California

"Simplicity of life is open to interpretation," admits Father Tim Reker. "The danger with those who define it too loosely is that all of a sudden the priesthood becomes another form of yuppie living. It makes your message less credible. It takes away from the nature of ministry, your availability, and the reason we are celibate. I find simplicity of life is a necessary corollary with celibacy and prayer. Those three things go together."

How a priest incorporates this concept of simple living into his daily life will vary. Some will drive inexpensive or older model cars. Some cut down on their living expenses. Some increase their donations to charities.

"I don't have a TV because if I had one I'd watch it. There are a lot of distractions in the world, and somehow, you have to prepare a place for yourself where you can meditate and study so when you interact with people you are solid in your very being. It's like eating junk food. If you're just absorbing junk literature and junk television, you're going to get sick." Father Gilio Dipre, Erie, Pennsylvania

Monsignor James Wall, a diocesan priest who serves as the Director of the St. Columban Center, a retreat house in Derby, New York, made a voluntary promise to live a life of poverty. His promise of poverty was a radical departure from the norm. Unlike a priest in a religious order, he still must provide for his retirement. He does not have to ask permission of anyone to buy something. He must judge for himself what constitutes poverty. He interprets poverty as a choice to live humbly and modestly.

"It calls for a healthy detachment from the material things of this world lest they ever deter me from entering into a deeper communion with God," he explains. "When I speak of communion with God, I am talking about worship and prayer, which strengthens my relationship with God, my creator and Lord. Should I allow material things to stand in the way of a deeper prayer life I would be failing in poverty. This promise of poverty also requires a sharing of my possessions to alleviate my brother's or sister's poverty state. Should I fail to be generous at such times, I would be failing to live poverty. Have I failed? Most certainly, yes. But the ideal I have chosen to accept as a way to God is precious to me. It is a daily challenge to live this ideal fully. To live the promise of poverty doesn't mean that one always succeeds, but that one never gives up trying to approach the ideal."

"I try to live simply, and I think most priests do. But I don't think we're going to be judged primarily on our poverty. I think we're going to be judged primarily on our love." Father Vincent O'Malley, CM, Niagara Falls, New York

"To love is the best thing about being a priest," says Father Emile Briere. "We're weak human beings. We're dealing sometimes with people who are a lot holier than we are. We have nothing except God's favor, his mercy, his love. God loves me. Therefore, I can love other people. I can sacrifice myself. I can be obedient. Love is the essence of Christianity. God loves me, and therefore, I can trust him."

In the sacrament of Holy Orders, a priest makes a supreme act of trust in God. It is a total surrender. It is literally laying down your life with the firm belief that God, who has begun the good work in you, will bring it to fulfillment.

Chapter Notes

"is never made to a bishop or religious superior personally...": Howard P. Bleichner, SS, Daniel Buechlein, OSB, Robert Leavitt, SS, *Celibacy for the Kingdom, Theological Reflections and Practical Perspectives.*

"Poverty or simplicity of life is a commitment...": Bryant, p. 68.

CHAPTER 13

You are a Priest Forever

"On the day of my ordination I can remember being very nervous. While I was listening to the word of God, I felt an incredible calm. Then I realized: I can't do this by myself, but with God, I can make this commitment, and I can try to be the best priest possible." Father Jim Bastian, Amherst, New York

"The opening hymn was, 'This is a victory for our God.' It was a day of victory. It was God's victory in me, because I had been away from the Church for twelve years before I experienced a conversion that brought me back to the faith in a powerful way." Father Don Guglielmi, East Haven, Connecticut

"In the sacristy before we went out, I felt cool as a cucumber. Walking down the aisle, I went into orbit. Then I entered into the mystery of priesthood. It was the greatest day of my life." Father Bob Fagan, Allentown, Pennsylvania

On the morning of ordination in the Diocese of Buffalo, the candidates gather in the front parlor of the Cathedral rectory. They are excited, nervous, and a little scared. Bishop Henry Mansell talks

129

with them briefly. "On behalf of the Diocese, I thank you for the commitment you make today," he says. "It is a thrilling day for the Church. You are richly gifted, and you are making a superb gift in return. May God bless you for all the years ahead."

Then, dressed in albs, they begin the procession into the cathedral where their families, friends, and fellow parishioners wait. During the Liturgy of the Word, the candidates sit with their families. Following the reading of the Gospel, the rector of the seminary presents them to the bishop.

"Do you judge them to be worthy?" Bishop Mansell asks.

"After inquiry among the people of God and upon the recommendation of those concerned with their training, I testify that they have been found worthy," the rector replies.

The bishop gives a homily. Then each candidate kneels before the bishop, placing his hands in the bishop's, and promising obedience to him and his successors. "May God who has begun the good work in you bring it to fulfillment," the bishop prays.

While everyone in the church intones the ancient Litany of Saints, the candidates lie prostrate on the altar. Then, Bishop Mansell invokes the Holy Spirit. The candidates rise, and one by one, in silence, they kneel before the bishop, who lays hands on them. This is the most sacred moment of the ordination. There is no sound in the cathedral.

"At this moment I think of the wondrous power of the Holy Spirit," admits Bishop Mansell. "From this day forward these men will be priests of God: ministers of the sacraments, servants, leaders. An awesome future begins to unfold, mysterious, exciting, sacred."

The newly ordained priests are vested in a stole and chasuble. Their hands are anointed. When the gifts of bread and wine are brought to the altar, the bishop tells them, "Accept from the holy people of God the gifts to be offered to Him. Know what you are doing, and imitate the mystery you celebrate: model your life on the mystery of the Lord's cross." Then, the Liturgy of the Eucharist begins.

"I was trying to pray through the whole ceremony. I remember weeping during the Litany of Saints. I remember the bishop's hands on my head. I remember having the vestments placed on me. I remember celebrating the Mass with the bishop. Talk about a defining moment. I just knew I was changed forever. It was a wonderful, happy, scary, awesome, bigger-than-me experience." Father Ted Jost, Tonawanda, New York

Some priests remember every moment of their ordination as if it were a video playback. Other priests are so nervous that they barely remember anything. For most priests, however, there are one or two special moments that remain permanently emblazoned in their hearts.

Some recall the procession into the church:

"As we walked into the vestibule, I remember hearing the music. I could see priests, family, friends, classmates. For the first time, I saw all the different parts of my life — growing up, high school, Newman Center, seminary, friends from Rome — and I was overwhelmed with the sense that this was the right thing to do. I felt very much at peace." Father Richard Siepka, East Aurora, New York

Some recall the moment when they were presented to the bishop:

"When the bishop asked whether the candidates were worthy to become priests, the entire church began to applaud. For me it was a great affirmation. I turned around and acknowledged all the people who supported me, who loved me, who wanted me to be a good priest. That was super meaningful. The community aspect of priesthood is so powerful." Father Jim Bastian, Amherst, New York

Many priests say the time that they are lying prostrate during the Litany of the Saints was a key moment:

"There I was, lying face down on the altar. Everyone in church was praying. I knew that I was very close to the culmination of many years of study, work, pain and worry. I was giving myself to God in a public ceremony. I was deeply moved and deeply aware of the fact that the power of Christ was going to come into me in a new way. I would be empowered to do what I would not be able to do otherwise." Father John Catoir, Paterson, New Jersey

Others say the most profound moment was kneeling before the bishop for the imposition of hands:

"I could feel the bishop's hands on my head. I knew that when I stood up, what was happening would be permanent and final. I also knew what it demanded of me. It was so incredibly awesome that I didn't know whether I could fulfill it. It was overpowering." Monsignor Paul Burkard, Orchard Park, New York

Sometimes the most poignant moment occurs after the ceremony. Monsignor John Madsen remembers a close friend waiting for him in the back of the church. "He told me that he had been waiting eight years for me to be ordained because he needed to go to confession and he wouldn't trust anyone else. So we went back inside the church and I heard his confession. This incident was extremely touching to me."

For some priests the day of ordination holds bittersweet memories because of the death of a loved one. Father David LiPuma lost both parents during his first year of the minor seminary:

My ordination took place in my home parish. I was born and raised there and had all my sacraments there. My parents were buried from there. After the ceremony, I remember blessing my grandmother and thinking how she'd been through all of this with me. I remember missing my parents very strongly that day, but I also had that strong feeling of their presence.

Two days after Father Ted Jost's ordination, a priest friend and mentor died after a long struggle with diabetes:

I was ordained on Saturday and said my first Mass on Sunday. He died on Monday. The Lord was teaching me about the paschal mystery. I went to St. John's University in New York to concelebrate the funeral. His sister told me, "I guess he figured he replaced himself so he could go to God."

Some priests are so nervous and excited that on some level they seem to lose touch with reality. "I left my car at the Cathedral after the ceremony because I forgot that I drove!" laughs Father Robert Wozniak.

The next day, when Father Wozniak celebrated his first Mass, he still felt nervous and distracted. He was surprised when a woman from the parish, who had lost almost all her sight, told him that throughout the Mass she felt a deep sense of peace.

"She had gone all over the country to cure the blindness, but nothing worked," he recalls. "The day after my first Mass, she had a simple procedure performed on her eyes, and she got her sight back. She credited it to the peace that she felt. You never know how God will touch people through you."

Many priests admit that they felt nervous during their first Mass:

"I was scared to say the words of the consecration for the first time. I was afraid of singing the Doxology. I was afraid that all the other priests singing in a different tone might mess me up. But all of a sudden, being part of that group of priests gave me an incredible feeling that I will never forget. There were twelve priests at my first Mass. It hit me that all of these priests, and all the priests and bishops before them had been doing this for almost two thousand years. Now I was part of that." Father Jim Bastian, Amherst, New York

Others say they felt an incredible sense of calm and a deep assurance that can only come from God:

"My first Mass was an ah-ha kind of confirming experience like, 'Yes, you can do it.' At the moment of the consecration, I can remember being focused. I wasn't worried about my hands or gestures. I just remember thinking, 'I'm celebrating this Mass and this is the Body of Christ.'" Father David LiPuma, Buffalo, New York

After the first Mass, there is usually a parish reception and the new priest blesses the people:

"When I had my first Mass, there was a general invitation in the bulletin to come. There had to be 3000 people. The reception was supposed to last from 5:30 to 8 p.m. I gave out blessings until 11:30 that night without a break. I could see people standing in line for hours. People did this out of personal love for me, but also out of love for the priesthood." Monsignor John Madsen, Depew, New York

The ordination, the first Mass, the receptions, the people, the blessings are all part of the wonder of the priesthood. But also important are the dreams a newly ordained priest holds for the future:

"For me, it was a dream and a hope that I would be a good parish priest. That was my only dream." Father Jim Bastian, Amherst, New York

"I wanted to reject mediocrity and lukewarmness, and be zealous for souls — for the good of the Church and for the glory of God." Father Don Guglielmi, East Haven, Connecticut

"My dreams as a newly ordained priest continue to live on: To help serve the poor, the elderly, the abandoned, the unloved. To help lead people back to a loving God. To champion social justice issues. To bring hope to the hopeless. The dream remains the cornerstone of my ministry." Father Robert Couto, Nashua, New Hampshire

CHAPTER 14

The Best Part of
Being a Priest

"The best part of being a priest is knowing that you have been chosen. It's knowing that you're not worthy, but that doesn't matter to God. For some mysterious reason, God has chosen you and that's awesome!" Father Bob Fagan, Allentown, Pennsylvania

"The best part of being a priest is the Mass. During Mass, you know that you are the instrument of the most powerful act that can be performed by any human being on earth. You stand in the person of Christ, and united with him, you offer to the Father, the perfect adoration, the perfect reparation, the perfect reconciliation, the perfect thanksgiving and the perfect intercession for every poor soul in the world. It helps everyone — the living, the dead, the souls in purgatory. You gather all those people and lift them to heaven." Father Emile Briere, Combermere, Ontario

"The best part is to be invited into people's lives at important times. It doesn't matter much who I am individually, but they want a priest there. It can be happy, joyful times or it can be tough times. It always amazes me how readily priests are invited into people's lives." Father Tim Reker, Winona, Minnesota

Father John Catoir boarded a cross-town bus in Manhattan one afternoon and sat down next to a very distinguished looking Hispanic woman. As soon as he sat down, the woman said, "Excuse me, but are you a Catholic priest?"

He said, "Yes."

"Father, do I have a fever?" she asked.

This sudden act of trust came as a shock to Father Catoir. He touched her face and she felt a little warm. He took her pulse and it was elevated enough for him to think she probably did have a fever.

"I think I'm coming down with something," she said, "and I'm going to have to fly home to Argentina tomorrow."

Father Catoir told her that the bus was heading toward Roosevelt Hospital. "I'll tell you when to get off," he said. "All you have to do is walk two blocks, and you'll be there. Go to the emergency room and tell them you have a fever."

"Oh, thank you, Father," she replied.

This scene could have been played out on any bus, train, or airplane with any person and any priest. "When you're wearing this black suit and the collar amazing things happen," Father Catoir says.

> "People see you as Christ. That's the most wonderful thing about the priesthood. When you walk into a hospital, or a church, or a restaurant, people identify you as an alter-Christus, another Christ. For me it's a humbling experience because I know who I really am with all my faults, limitations, and sinfulness." Father Ted Jost, Tonawanda, New York

"Vatican II reminds us that the priest ministers to people in Christ's name by teaching, by making holy and by leading," explains Bishop Paul Loverde. "There are many other things we do, but those three things — teaching, making holy, and leading — are central. The real role of a priest is to be Christ the teacher, Christ the sanctifier, and Christ the leader. It's very interesting that theologians might emphasize one aspect, like Christ who is the Word, so the priest's central role is to preach, but they are very careful to always include the other two which are sacrament and leadership. Another might emphasize the sacramental role, but are very careful to include teaching and leadership. Sometimes they emphasize the servant-leader role. I would say that in the future, the priest will be the person who acts in the person of Christ Jesus in preaching the word, in teaching, in celebrating the sacraments, in making holy, and in leading God's people."

Many priests agree that it is in sacramental moments that their priesthood is affirmed in very powerful ways:

"I can't tell you too much because it was a confessional experience. It was an individual who came to me after wrestling with a problem for over three decades. When I heard the problem, I thought, 'What am I going to tell this person?' Then all of a sudden, something came out. There were tears, and absolution, and a deep sense of peace. I remember thinking afterward, 'Where did those words come from?' I thought of the Scripture passage where it says don't worry about what to say because the Holy Spirit will inspire you (Mt 10:20)." Father Richard Siepka, East Aurora, New York

For some priests, the presence of God becomes most powerful when they anoint someone who is dying or when they preside at a funeral:

"I remember going to the hospital to see a young man who was dying from AIDS. I remember thinking, 'This is tough. Will he receive me?' I remember praying hard that this boy would listen to me, and we would be able to talk.
When I got to his room, he was alone. He was not upset that I was there. He told me his whole story. I asked if he would like absolution, and he said, 'I'd like that.'
I told him I am a great believer in the Lord's anointing and healing. 'I'd like that,' he said. So I anointed him.
I asked if he could forgive the Church for the way he had

been treated in the past. He said, 'I can forgive if you are the Church.' I was really moved. I told him he was a beautiful young man.

The following Thursday, I brought him Communion. The next day, he took a turn for the worse. I went to the hospital. He was gasping for breath. I said, 'John, let go. Jesus is waiting. It's going to be a wonderful experience. There's no more hassle. Jesus loves you. Let go.'

The whole family was there, and we started to say the Lord's Prayer. I held his head in the crook of my arm. He died just like that. It was a moment of ministry that was really touching." Monsignor William Stanton, Buffalo, New York

Some priests say they watch in awe as God unexpectedly touches a person's life in a profound way:

"I had someone in a counseling situation who had a long history of being abused. In the middle of our conversation, this person's eyes suddenly opened to God's presence and something happened. I think there was a new hope there that wasn't apparent before." Monsignor Paul Burkard, Orchard Park, New York

Other priests point to the power of prayer:

"I had been a priest for 20 years and had never really prayed with anyone. We were not trained to do that. After I asked the Lord for the gift of prayer, I found myself thrown into situations where there didn't seem to be anything else to do but pray. The first time I prayed with anyone was with a girl who hadn't slept for five weeks. She came to school the next day and thanked me because she had slept soundly the night before. I walked away from that encounter dazed. I thought, 'What is this? The power of suggestion?' Then I realized that it was the power of God." Father Bob Bedard, Ottawa, Ontario

"These kinds of things happen frequently and they really can't be explained except that it is the power of God and the power of prayer," says Bishop Henry Mansell. "I've seen people healed from very serious illnesses. Doctors couldn't define it, but there was very powerful prayer going on. There was no other answer but the power of prayer and the Spirit working in our lives."

> "Witnessing God's power in other people's lives is the best part of being a priest. If I can step back and know that I have nothing to do with what is going on, and watch God's power in someone else's life, it's a wonderful thing." Father Ron Cafeo, Combermere, Ontario

Moral theologian, Father Bernard Häring, CSSR, warns that priests should never attribute any kind of miraculous powers to themselves by virtue of ordination. "There is nothing miraculous or magical about us," he explains. "On the other hand, God does great things in and through those who, like Mary, live a life of praise and abiding trust. True to our calling, we are nothing more and nothing less than humble co-workers with God who are open to receive God's graciousness to effect healing in all our relationships with God, others, and all of creation. The starting point is always our realization that we, too, are in constant need of healing; we, too, are in need of the ongoing advance of God's gracious encouraging love and presence. At our very best, we are nothing short of wounded healers. In the measure that we unflinchingly encourage and trust others, this trust and encouragement flows back to us as healing and strengthening power."

Many years ago, someone asked Catherine de Hueck Doherty, "What is a priest?" Without saying a word, she picked up a pencil and wrote:

> A priest is a lover of God,
> a priest is a lover of men,
> a priest is a holy man
> because he walks before the face of the All-Holy.

A priest understands all things,
a priest forgives all things,
a priest encompasses all things.

The heart of a priest is pierced, like Christ's,
with the lance of love.

The heart of a priest is open, like Christ's,
for the whole world to walk through.

The heart of a priest is a vessel of compassion,
the heart of a priest is a chalice of love,
the heart of a priest is the trysting place
of human and divine love.

A priest is a man whose goal is to be another Christ;
a priest is a man who lives to serve.

A priest is a man who has crucified himself
so that he too may be lifted up
and draw all things to Christ.

A priest is a man in love with God.

A priest is the gift of God to man
and of man to God.

A priest is the symbol of the Word made flesh,
a priest is the naked sword of God's justice,
a priest is the hand of God's mercy,
a priest is the reflection of God's love.

Nothing can be greater in this world than a priest,
nothing but God himself.

"The best part of being a priest is knowing that you're sharing in the greatest adventure in the universe — the sanctification and salvation of the world," admits Father Don Guglielmi. "Every time you offer the Mass you're in union with all the angels and saints, the entire Church worships the Father, and the whole world is raised up. More concretely, it is the daily realization that you are putting into practice Gospel love for people. To see people turn to God is the greatest satisfaction. You know that you're just a poor humble instrument and God is using you in the greatest of all missions."

What's good about being a priest is wonderful and warm and inspiring. But that's not the whole story. The priesthood can also be difficult and demanding.

Chapter Notes

"There is nothing miraculous or magical about us...": Häring, pp. 20-21.

Many years ago, someone asked Catherine de Hueck Doherty... and f.: Catherine de Hueck Doherty, *Dear Father*, Combermere, Ontario: Madonna House Publications, 1988, pp. 1-2.

CHAPTER 15

The Hardest Part
of Being a Priest

"The hardest part of being a priest is when you see that despite your best efforts people don't respond. You want to set hearts on fire for the love of God. You reach out to people and say, 'God is love. Love him back. It is the greatest adventure in the world. It is the most exciting thing in the world. It is worth any amount of suffering. Don't be afraid.' In spite of that, people pull away. That's the hardest part." Father Don Guglielmi, East Haven, Connecticut

"The hardest part is not being able to take away the pain and hurt experienced by so many. It's not being able to change the societal ills and injustices. It's balancing limited time and expertise with trying to meet many needs." Father Robert Couto, Nashua, New Hampshire

"Just as you're present during great moments of grace, there are also 'Cross' moments for a priest when the only thing you have to hold onto is the Lord. It can be when you have to say no to someone or when you have to tell a family that their father is dying. It can happen when you're preaching to people who don't want to hear a word that you say. The 'Cross' moments include the times when you want someone to hold you, but you stand there alone and know

that the Lord is holding you. Those are the tough parts of
the priesthood." Father Joseph Gatto, East Aurora, New
York

When the family of an elderly man, who was dying, asked if
he wanted to talk to a priest, the man replied, "Yes, but don't call
that Monsignor at Sts. Peter and Paul!"

"They called me," admits Monsignor David Gallivan, "and
delicately told me about their father's wish."

Monsignor Gallivan tried to find another priest, but he had
no luck on such short notice. When he called the family back, they
asked him to come anyway because their father was in such a state
that he probably would no longer recognize him.

"I anointed him," Monsignor Gallivan recalls, "and we had a
moving prayer experience with the family around his bed. My of-
fense never came up. If he recognized me, all was forgiven. To this
day I have no recollection of ever having met the man previously,
let alone having offended him."

It takes a lot of humility to be a priest. But that's not all it takes.
In anyone's life, there are good times, bad times, and what Father
Joseph Gatto referred to as "Cross" moments.

Father John Catoir agrees: "Everyone wants to talk about love,
but no one wants to talk about the cross. Wherever you have love,
you have a cross. Wherever you have a cross, you have a victim.
Wherever you have a cross, you also have a resurrection, but it's
usually so far down the road that all you see are the nails."

What are some of the crosses in the lives of most priests?

• Dealing with people's demands

Most priests will say the best part of the priesthood is the
people, but people also rank high as one of the most difficult parts
of the priesthood. Sometimes, it's a matter of people loving you so
much that they begin to put demands on you.

"Lots of people love you and lots of people are generous and kind. Lots of people want to spend time with you and do things with you. But sometimes, you find yourself discerning whether they want a relationship with a Roman collar or whether they really like the person beneath the collar! Sometimes, you get close to people and they want you to always be there, but you can't always be there. There are times when you enjoy their company, but then you have times when you want to be alone, and you pull away. It's the struggle with interpersonal relationships and drawing the lines. That's one of the greatest challenges." Father David LiPuma, Buffalo, New York

• Dealing with difficult people

Sometimes, people are a lot like the nursery rhyme about the little girl with the little curl: When they are good, they are very, very good. And when they are bad they are horrid!

"The hardest part for me is what I'm going through right now in the parish. The people don't get along very well with each other and that bothers me. I guess I have an expectation of the Christian community that people would try to be supportive of one another, but what you see sometimes are people in a parish guarding their turf or trying to build turf for themselves. You see people who are jealous. You see people who want to head up committees because it affords them some kind of prestige. Working with people who are not in ministry for the right reasons is difficult. None of us goes into ministry with pure motivation, but when it's so obvious, and people don't get along, you can actually see the destruction caused by people acting against one another. I would say that's the most difficult thing. But I feel as though I can't let up. I have to grit my teeth and keep going. I almost feel embattled. I don't like that feeling. I don't think that's what Church is all about. But right now, for this parish community, I believe it's what leadership is all about. If I don't become a stabilizing influence here, this parish could self-destruct." Monsignor John Madsen, Depew, New York

• Fear of hurting people unintentionally

Priests today understand the woundedness and insecurity of people. They also know that people have different personalities and are looking for different things in a priest. As a result, some priests are conscious of their ability to accidentally slight people or hurt their feelings.

> "I pray for the people that I might hurt by a simple action, a joke, or teasing. It might be something that you did very naturally, but they say, 'Look at what this priest did to me!' That is one of the most difficult things about being a priest. People make generalizations about the whole Church based on who I am." Father Jim Bastian, Amherst, New York

• Saying no

Priests also face the reality that they can't make everyone happy all of the time. They have to uphold Church teachings or policies which may be unpopular. Sometimes, they have to say no.

> "Saying no is very difficult. You have to follow the rules of the Church and sometimes that's hard. Sometimes people aren't reasonable, either. When you have to say no, you should do it with a lot of tenderness and compassion. For example, when someone comes to have their baby baptized because that's what they do in their family, but there's no faith expression, you have to be able to say, 'Why do you want the baby baptized? If you come to me, you have a responsibility to raise that baby as a Catholic.' Those things are hard. But the joys overcome those things most of the time for me." Monsignor William Stanton, Buffalo, New York

• **Trying to incorporate new ideas into a parish**

Young priests often come out of the seminary on fire with new ideas for liturgy, music, prayer experiences and new ministries. One of their biggest disappointments is finding that some people are not interested in new ideas and stubbornly refuse to accept change.

> "I got the idealism knocked out of me when I went to my first assignment. It was a country parish with 57 Irish families. They said, 'We have only one thing to say to you. We have one Communion breakfast a year. We have no societies. We have no adult education. Don't bother because we won't come to that stuff.' It was true. I tried it and they didn't!" Monsignor John Madsen, Depew, New York

• **Lack of respect for the priesthood**

In the past, priesthood in the United States was prestigious. But over the past 25 years, the image of priests has changed. "The intense focus in recent years on clerical celibacy and sexuality has contributed to a diminishing respect for the priesthood and made priests themselves feel more vulnerable," says Father Thomas P. Rausch, SJ. "So have recent scandals and revelations about pedophilic priests."

> "Priesthood has been slammed around a lot because of the misdeeds of some priests so you're always suspect. A few years ago when there was so much in the press, it was almost embarrassing to go out in religious attire. You felt like you were targeting yourself. People were suspicious of you." Father Ron Pecci, OFM, Holy Name Province

Father Bernard Häring, CSSR, suggests that priests today carry deep wounds from the past as well as the present. "If we allow ourselves to recognize and acknowledge our great woundedness and our status of being retarded and handicapped in so many ways, our very deficiencies may well turn out to be God's gracious blessing in disguise," he says. "We might very well become signs and symbols of the disfigured Servant of God: 'Here is my servant whom I uphold, my chosen in whom my soul delights' (Isaiah 42:1). 'Many were astonished at him, so marred was his appearance' (Isaiah 52:14). 'He was despised and rejected by others; a man of sufferings and acquainted with infirmity; and as one from whom others hide their faces' (Isaiah 53:3)."

• Getting wounded in the war between conservatives and liberals

The battle lines are clearly drawn in today's Church between conservatives and liberals. On the right, you have groups who monitor what priests say and write letters to Rome. On the left, you have groups who challenge Church positions and gather signatures on petitions.

Some priests align themselves with the warring camps. Others find themselves caught in the middle with both sides firing at them.

> "When I was growing up, I'm sure there were some issues going on with the bishops and the priests, but by and large, I never heard or did not know that Father, in the pulpit, having given this sermon or homily, could be called down to the bishop's office. Now it can happen." Father Paul Golden, CM, Niagara University

What's frustrating to some priests is that their words are often taken out of context or misinterpreted. The tendency to stereotype makes things even worse. "Conservative" priests are often accused of being unfeeling and legalistic. "Liberal" priests are often accused of being unloyal and heretical. As a result, one priest includes the following request in every talk he gives: "If you disagree with something I say tonight, please have the courtesy to tell me so I'll at least know what the issue is."

In his opening address at the U.S. Catholic Bishops meeting in November 1997, Bishop Anthony M. Pilla warned that a Church, which is not at peace within itself, acts as a countersign. He focused on four areas where reconciliation is needed:

- in matters involving liturgy
- in public discussion of issues in the Church
- in response to those who have been hurt by someone in the Church
- in resolving the polarization around matters of doctrine and authoritative teaching.

He criticized those "very angry voices who apparently feel justified in using a rhetoric of violence towards whoever disagrees with them."

He urged Catholics to preserve the clarity of the faith, but warned that truth must be spoken with love. "In this sense, even with issues of doctrine, we must try to talk not across a chasm but side by side."

"Internal fighting in the Church hurts everyone. It's unfortunate, and it plays against the need for flexibility and openness on both sides. The more progressive have to be open to the traditions, and the traditional have to be open to the fact that the Church is a living organism that needs to grow and change. I respect greatly the seminarians today because they have to face all of this in their own lives. I think we must begin to recognize the need to come together. Polarization can become so broad that we can have two realities that are not speaking to each other. It's a real concern because it threatens the unity in the Church." Father Richard Siepka, East Aurora, New York

• Dealing with administrative details

Priests are trained to celebrate the sacraments, preach the word of God, and minister to the needs of the people, but too often they end up pouring most of their energy into worrying about whether the boiler is going to last through the winter, the cost of utilities, the leak in the roof, the holes in the gutters, and how to raise money to pay for all of this.

> "Right now, the hardest thing for me is the crazy administration stuff. You know you can and probably should be doing something pastoral, but you have to keep the ship afloat. It takes time and energy to do the nitty-gritty stuff. You do it because you have to. It's not a lot of fun. There's an element of challenge in terms of can you do it and can you make it happen, but it's less enjoyable and less fulfilling than the times you're with people and you're doing things to help people live and celebrate their lives."
> Monsignor Paul Burkard, Orchard Park, New York

Many priests today admit that priesthood in the future must be more focused. Celebrating sacraments and preaching will remain essential functions of the parish priest, but priests may have to turn over the day to day administrative responsibilities to parish staff or a business manager. The trend toward collaborative ministry with groups of parishes working together to provide adult education or sacramental preparation is already emerging in many parts of the country.

"It is evident to most people in Church work that the old paradigm of parish life, that which consists mostly of programs and organizations with clergy and professional staff doing direct delivery, is dysfunctional and is no longer effective," writes Father Patrick Brennan. "What is not clear to many people is what the *new* paradigm is or what it will look like. Yet there seems to be a growing consensus that the key ingredient of the new paradigm has something to do with community or communion, with people united with one another and God."

• Dealing with the parish staff

Tensions can also arise between priests and the parish staff. Since the Second Vatican Council, involvement of trained lay people in parish ministries has mushroomed. In the United States, Catholic parishes now employ 26,000 lay ministers for 20 or more hours a week. For some priests it's a challenge. For others it's an opportunity.

> "It can be a problem for a priest if he doesn't know how to work with people. He can feel threatened by it. In the past, we were basically trying to run the show ourselves, but as your vision for ministry broadens and grows in the Church, you see most of the gifts for pastoral ministry lie within lay people. Clergy have very specific roles to play in pastoring, fathering, encouraging, preaching, teaching, and administering the sacraments. As far as running every meeting, every ministry, every outreach, it is impossible. When you learn to work with a team of lay people, you realize how rich that can be." Father Bob Bedard, Ottawa, Ontario

In *Transforming Parish Ministry: The Changing Roles of Catholic Clergy, Laity and Women Religious,* Jay P. Dolan, R. Scott Appleby, Patricia Byrne and Debra Campbell admit that part of the difficulty with the influx of lay ministers is that it subjected priests to a new level of scrutiny:

> Was he as *au courant* about the latest trends in parish worship as the Sister who had taken a graduate degree in liturgical studies? Was he as knowledgeable about Church history as the lay historian teaching adult education courses in the parish?
> The experience of collaborating with gifted and intelligent women as equals was new and challenging to those priests who attempted it. It was also confusing, as were several elements of the lay ministry explosion.
> If the priest did in fact learn to collaborate, he remained ultimately responsible by canon law for the welfare of the

parish and answerable on this score to his bishop. How was he — must he — to retain this "bottom-line" mentality in a collegial setting? And if he accepted in principle the plurality of spirit-filled ministries, how was he to articulate his own distinctiveness as an ordained priest?

Priests today continue to struggle with these questions, but a recent study of seminarians showed that while they recognized these challenges, they believed one way to prepare for the future is to "increase their own education, deepen their spirituality, be more open to learning from others, and improve their collaborative efforts."

• Trying to keep a sense of balance

The constant demands on a priest make it very easy to slip into unhealthy patterns of workaholism which lead to burnout. In their essay on the priesthood, Archbishop Daniel Buechlein, OSB, Howard P. Bleichner, SS, and Robert Leavitt, SS, emphasized that "good exercise, interesting reading, a concern for cultivating one's mind, a taste for art and music are not merely leisure-time activities. They represent significant ways of engaging the body, mind and spirit. If we are rightly engaged, we will be happier and prayer will become easier too."

"In the seminary, they would talk about what the schedule would be like as a parish priest: You'll be up early. You'll go crazy all morning. In the afternoon it will slow down a little. Then dinner and the evening is crazy again. Sometimes you'll go until 10 at night. Sometimes you'll need to take a nap in the afternoon. They explained that to us, and it's true. You have to adjust your lifestyle." Father Ted Jost, Tonawanda, New York

• **Rectory living**

Some priests say rectory living is one of the most challenging parts of the priesthood:

> "You live in the place where you work. It's like living in the fire hall. Not only that, but you have three meals a day with people you might not ordinarily want to have a cup of coffee with. I think rectory life can be one of the most difficult things." Father John Mergenhagen, Derby, New York

For diocesan priests, frustration with rectory life is nothing new. "In the old days, the heaviest cross of a young curate was dealing with a grumpy, old pastor and the housekeeper, who enforced the rules," says Father Emile Briere.

Monsignor William Stanton agrees. "Our spiritual director in the seminary used to say, 'If your pastor says, "It's raining cow flops from the barn," you say, "Yes, Father, and damn big ones!"'"

There are still situations today where young priests struggle with cantankerous pastors. "Sometimes, priests find themselves trying to mediate between the policies of the pastor and the needs of the people," admits Father Edmund Lane, SSP. "Sometimes pastors are jealous or intolerant of their associates. It can be very difficult."

Today, most pastors strive for good communication with their associates. In many rectories, pastors try to foster a greater sense of community, support, and shared ministry:

> "If we're both in for dinner, my current pastor and I pray together and then have dinner. It works out fine. We're like family. We need each other." Father Ted Jost, Tonawanda, New York

With the decreasing number of clergy, however, too many priests find that the greatest struggle in rectory life involves learning to live alone. They face the challenge of learning how to pray alone, to eat alone, and to develop some form of rest, relaxation, and recreation.

> "That's what we keep hearing all the time. Priests are liv-
> ing alone. Even priests who do live with more than one in
> a rectory are not necessarily living in community. They live
> their own lives and share a building." John Fletcher, Ot-
> tawa, Ontario

"Rectory life needs to be studied and evaluated," says Father Jude Brady, OSB, of St. Mary's, Pennsylvania. "Viable alternatives to the traditional concept need to be offered to the ordained priest."

In the Archdiocese of Ottawa, a group of priests and seminarians have already started to institute a new vision of shared priestly life called Companions of the Cross. It began as a prayer-support group with one priest and three seminarians in 1984. "We met faithfully every week," recalls Father Roger Vandenakker. "We found that the experience was tremendous in terms of personal support, faith sharing, and our ability to pray together. We felt this great unity and bonding in the Spirit. During that first year the sense began to unfold that God was calling us to form a community. It came in three stages. First, there was the sense that the Lord wanted this group to endure beyond our seminary years into the priesthood. The second sense was that we were not only to be a personal support for each other, but we should find ways to minister together in team ministry. The third sense was that the Lord was calling us to actually live together."

In 1988, Archbishop Joseph-Aurele Plourde gave the Companions of the Cross canonical status as a public association of the faithful. They hope to eventually be erected as a Society of Apostolic Life. Some say their efforts at community living will serve as one of the new models for diocesan priesthood in the next millennium.

• **Fear of the future**

Researchers predict a 65 percent increase in the number of Catholics and a 40 percent drop in the number of diocesan priests in the United States as we move into the twenty-first century. In the next ten years, the Catholic Church in the United States will lose 950 priests a year to resignations, retirements and death. We will gain only 650 new priests a year. "By the year 2005," researchers predict, "there would be 2,200 parishioners for each priest in contrast with 1,100 parishioners per priest in 1966."

No one really knows what this will mean. Some priests feel apprehensive about the future. They fear that they will become circuit riders, who go from parish to parish celebrating sacraments, but not really touching the lives of people.

Some of the younger priests and seminarians find it demoralizing to see so few men who are willing to embrace a priestly vocation. Some search for some deeper meaning in the vocation crisis:

> "People who are looking at the priesthood are asking why there aren't more people in the seminary. That's crossed my mind, too. What am I getting myself into? But I said that about Christianity. What am I getting myself into? Jesus Christ died on a cross. When you look at it from that point of view it makes it more important. There is some conviction. This is what I believe I am called to do. This is counter cultural. To follow Christ completely is not what everyone wants to do." Paul MacNeil, St. Catharine's, Ontario

Others feel that greater effort needs to be made to invite young men to take a serious look at the priesthood:

> "In Colombia, priests call everyone to work towards vocations, even my parents, my family. Here, only one person is working towards vocations. That is wrong. The other thing is that the seminarians here don't go to schools and colleges in the diocese and say, 'I am happy to be a semi-

narian. I am happy to pursue my priesthood.' In Colombia, we are on a team with two or three seminarians. We find time to go out and tell people who we are. God doesn't get tired from calling. We get tired." Juan Carlos Lasso, Raleigh, North Carolina

Another tough reality for many young priests is that the declining number of vocations makes it difficult to find priest friends in their own age group:

"Classmates are one piece that's missing for me. There are so few of us from all over the place that it's tough to find someone your age to click with. We just had an assembly five weeks ago and I was one of the youngest priests there. I started thinking: 'Where is most of the energy here?' It was going toward wellness, retirement, and other age issues. I was just ordained. But these other guys are in a whole different time of their lives. That's why friendships are very important to me. I have a very good friend in California who was in the novitiate with me. I have another priest here, who is just five years older, and we're really good friends. I keep trying to make those friendships work." Father Kevin Creagh, CM, Niagara Falls, New York

• Loneliness

Father John Merganhagan remembers watching a young priest after the wedding of a friend walk across the parking lot alone. "Priests do live with aloneness," he says. "Most priests have to come to grips with that."

"Even though I am very much a loner type person, I still need the company of brother priests once in a while. Loneliness is always lurking around the corner, and we need to help one another. Without each other, we literally die on the vine. Without these friendships, we suffer tremendously. It can literally be the difference between keeping or losing one's vocation." Father Paul Bombadier, Ware, Massachusetts

Bishop Paul Loverde agrees: "I think with the decreasing number of priests, it's a call to those of us who are priests, and those of us who are going to be priests, to depend on each other and develop more deeply those bonds of real fraternity and priestly support," he says. "When I freely give up my right to have my own family, in God's providence, I acquire a right to have another family which is a community of priests. Many priests really do care for each other and I am very touched by that."

"One of the great blessings of my life has been priest friends. You need someone with whom you can share the deep beliefs of your heart and your faith. I don't like going around and talking about my faith with just anybody. Our Lord had those kind of friends. It's very important." Father Gilio Dipre, Erie, Pennsylvania

Since 1971, Father Michael Scanlon, TOR, has met every week with a group of Franciscan friars. "The group has changed in membership over the years, but it has been an anchor in my life," he admits. "My brothers in the group know me. They know my joys and sorrows. They have heard my life story in some detail. They know where I have succeeded and where I have failed. They know about my desires, my hopes, my sins, my temptations. I tell them about my prayer life. They monitor the condition of my soul.

"I also bring all my important and difficult decisions to the group, along with any sense I have about what direction to go with them. When they confirm a direction, I feel empowered to go ahead and pursue it, and make whatever commitments it entails. The brothers take a personal concern for me. They tell me when I look tired and need to get away for a while. I do the same for them. This is the Church in action."

Father Emile Briere agrees. "The friendship of priests is absolutely essential to my perseverance and my happiness," he says. "You need guys you can really talk with and get the stuff off your chest. Fellow priests as friends are the greatest help in persevering. I've had very hard moments of trials and difficulties. After God, it's always been a priest friend who pulled me through."

In many places, priests form support groups. When Father Ron Pecci, OFM, was transferred to a new parish, the local diocesan priests invited him to join their Emmaus group. "I wasn't familiar with the program," he admits. "They told me it was a priestly support group that meets together once a month for dinner. We pray, talk about timely topics, and just be together. I thought it was a nice invitation. They were good men. I respected and admired them. Right now, there are seven of us, and there are things I might bring to that group that I might not talk about with the friars I live with. These men are not necessarily my best friends. My closest friends are Franciscans who live in different places. The Emmaus group has come together because of the ministry and the work. I'm glad they asked me to join."

Part of the loneliness priests face is not having their own family. "That's personally hard for me," says Father Richard Siepka. "I'm close to my nieces, but the sacrifice of not having my own family is always there."

Father Ted Jost agrees: "The one thing that's harder than not having a relationship with a woman is not having children," he says. "Sometimes a little one will grab your legs and hug you. I really sense Christ's presence at those moments. When those children come running to me, it's like God saying, 'These are the children I've given you. Love them as you would love your own.'"

• To constantly empty yourself so God can work through you

Most priests admit that one of the greatest struggles in becoming an instrument of God is the kenosis or stripping of oneself that must take place on an ongoing basis.

"To be a priest you have to lose yourself completely. That's very difficult because you want to be who you are. You want to think that you've got the talent and you've got the gifts. You don't have anything really. It's not me that works in someone's life. It's God. I've sat with people who are dying. I've sat with people who are suffering in jail. I sat next to a man during his trial and he sobbed through the whole thing. I knew when I was sitting next to him there was nothing I could do. I knew what the outcome was going to be. I knew he was going to be locked up. I couldn't even touch him to console him. But the person of Jesus Christ was doing something through me. Something was pouring into him by my presence, and it was enhanced by the fact that I felt totally inadequate. To witness that kind of thing is a tremendous gift, but it is also pain." Father Ron Cafeo, Combermere, Ontario

"To be a good priest is a real challenge," admits Father Thomas P. Rausch, SJ. "It is not an easy life. It is a genuine vocation which demands the kind of commitment that can only be lived out with the help of God's grace. It is a vocation to be a leader precisely in the way that Jesus was, as one who serves. The priest is a servant of God's wounded people. The Church today desperately needs this kind of servant leader."

It takes a lot of faith to be a servant leader. Monsignor David Gallivan and his 26-year-old nephew were camping in the Grand Canyon when the topic of faith arose.

"Without much thought, I shared a raw synthesis of my faith life," Monsignor Gallivan recalls. "It went something like this:

In my life, as in everyone's there are joys and tragedies, times of deep sharing and intimacy, but also almost unbearable loneliness. Sometimes we are rightfully proud of an accomplishment, but there come moments when we would rather disappear out of shame. While we can be exceedingly kind, at times our biting words, our apathy and our attitudes are harmful and destructive to others. Like St. Paul, we seem to do what we know is evil and avoid doing what we know is right. It's as if there were a war being

waged within us. One week we are in control of everything
— our work, our emotions, our sexuality, our finances, our
health, our family. Then, suddenly, we lose it. We don't
understand it completely. We need a glue, an overarching
reality, a divine relationship which holds it (and me) all
together. I call it faith. Without it, there is no logic, sense
or coherence to my life. Jesus and the Gospels are the only
sources in my life that consistently have something to say
to my joys and sorrows, my hopes and my disappointments.
Hence, my faith. It knits my life experiences together.

"The stars, the place and the company made me say those
things," Monsignor Gallivan admits. "My nephew said it was the
kind of homily he'd like to hear in church. Come to think of it, it's
the kind of homily I'd like to give."

Chapter Notes

"*Was he as* au courant *about the latest trends...*": Jay P. Dolan, R. Scott Appleby, Patricia Byrne
and Debra Campbell, *Transforming Parish Ministry: The Changing Roles of Catholic Clergy,
Laity and Women Religious,* New York: Crossroad, 1990, p. 100.

"*increase their own education, deepen their spirituality...*": *Seminarians in the Nineties, A National Study of
Seminarians in Theology,* p. 8.

"*Good exercise, interesting reading...*": Howard P. Bleichner, SS, Daniel Buechlein, OSB, Robert
Leavitt, SS, *Celibacy for the Kingdom, Theological Reflections and Practical Perspectives.*

"*The intense focus in recent years on clerical celibacy...*": Rausch, p. 44.

"*If we allow ourselves to recognize and acknowledge...*": Häring, p. 137.

In his opening address at the U.S. Catholic Bishops meeting... and f.: Jerry Filteau, "Pilla Address
Opens Meeting," *Catholic News Service,* November 10, 1997.

"*It is evident to most people in church work...*": Patrick J. Brennan, *Re-Imagining Evangelization,* New
York: Crossroad, 1995, p. 51.

"*Rectory life needs to be studied and evaluated...*": Jude Brady, OSB, "The Holy — and Healthy —
Rectory," *The Priest,* April, 1997.

Researchers predict a 65 percent increase in the number of Catholics..." and f.: Richard A. Schoenherr
and Lawrence A. Young, *Full Pews & Empty Altars: Demographics of the Priest Shortage in United
States Catholic Dioceses,* University of Wisconsin Press, 1993, p. xvii.

"*The group has changed in membership over the years...*" and f.: Scanlon, pp. 58-59.

"*To be a good priest is a real challenge...*": Rausch, p. 45.

CHAPTER 16

Could You Ever Become a Catholic Priest?

✝

"About ten months ago, I began to consider a vocation to the priesthood. Today, I am applying to the seminary and hope to begin my studies in January. I've had good times and bad times. There are moments when it is very clear to me that I should become a priest. There are trying moments as well. I looked at myself to see who I was and what experiences I've had. I found that I was indeed leaning toward the priesthood all my life." Nicholas Zientarski, Smithtown, New York

"I definitely don't deserve it, but God willing, I could become a priest. It's going to come to the point where I have to ask myself, 'How can I most fully follow Jesus?' There will be sacrifices in the priestly life, but I think I could do that." Mark Mambretti, Williamsville, New York

"Anyone who thinks he has this calling has an obligation to pursue it and not look back. The Lord will stop you if it is not what he intends." Jason Vidmar, Davenport, Iowa

When Father Gary Bagley was still a seminarian, he met a sociologist from Australia, who had come to the United States on

161

a teaching sabbatical. "He asked me and two other seminarians a very simple question," Father Bagley recalls. "Why do you want to be a priest?"

The first seminarian said he really wanted to be a teacher and help people understand the Scriptures, and morality, and the meaning of life. The second seminarian said he wanted to help people who were wounded and hurting.

"I took the angle of celebrating sacraments," Father Bagley admits. "I was pretty sure that I had come up with the third place answer. So I was pleasantly surprised when the sociologist said that all three answers were good, but I was the only one who needed to be ordained to do what I wanted to do. The other two could be very good teachers, healers, social workers, and counselors in any other profession. They didn't have to be ordained to do those things."

Technically, that's true. You can be a teacher, a preacher, a healer, a social worker, a counselor and a leader in a Christian community without becoming a priest. Yet, ordination raises all of these things that priests do to a different level. Pope John Paul II emphasizes that a priest becomes a sharer in many different life choices, sufferings and joys, disappointments and hopes:

"In every situation, his task is to show God to man as the final end of his personal existence. The priest becomes the one to whom people confide the things most dear to them and their secrets, which are sometimes very painful. He becomes the one whom the sick, the elderly and the dying wait for, aware that only he, a sharer in the priesthood of Christ, can help them in the final journey which is to lead them to God. As a witness to Christ, the priest is the messenger of man's supreme vocation to eternal life in God. And while he accompanies his brothers and sisters, he prepares himself: the exercise of the ministry enables him to deepen his own vocation to give glory to God in order to have a share in eternal life. He thus moves forward toward the day when Christ will say to him: 'Well done, good and faithful servant... enter into the joy of your master' (Mt 25:21)."

"I don't know if young people really see the priesthood as a radical commitment, but that's what it is," says Father David LiPuma.

"I am from Colombia where there are still plenty of vocations, but vocations there are very different than here. There is more materialism here. In Colombia, a vocation means giving back something to God. I believe this is lacking in America." Juan Carlos Lasso, Raleigh, North Carolina

Recent studies show that the men most interested in a vocation to the priesthood are attracted by the sense of mission and the willingness to make a personal sacrifice for God and others. In a study of priests ordained ten to thirty years, researchers discovered that successful, effective priests have twelve major characteristics in common:

• They are risk takers. They look at life with enthusiasm and thrive on change.
• They have a sense of balance and perspective, see themselves in relationship to a larger reality, have the ability to laugh at themselves, and to manage their time with an understanding that they have to take care of their own needs as well as the needs of others.
• They place great emphasis on being authentic, honest, and accountable with people and with Church authorities.
• They develop multiple close relationships with other priests and religious, family members and lay people.
• They see great significance in the priesthood and the mystery of God's call to preach the Gospel.
• They are sustained by the conviction that God is love and that God is with them always and constantly showering them with grace.

• They firmly believe that Jesus Christ is their role model and mentor. They operate on the premise: "What would Jesus do?" The death and resurrection of Christ gives them meaning in their own lives.

• They maintain an active spiritual life through prayer, Scripture and liturgy.

• They believe that God is working behind the scenes and they tap into the deeper reality of God's presence in daily life.

• They become energized by the people they serve. They draw inspiration from the lives of people. They are awed by their role in people's lives at key moments such as birth, death, sickness and suffering.

• They are good listeners. They find that listening helps them serve the needs of others.

• They are sensitive to people's needs. They use their personal talents to help others. They see priesthood as an opportunity to serve and to lead. They see themselves as servant leaders.

For Father Joe Rogliano, the decision to become a priest solidified while he was in the seminary:

> I became a priest because I thought it best matched who I am with how I can best utilize who I am. I think God called me to serve him and to make him more accessible to people. In a nutshell, I became a priest because I think that's where I'm supposed to be. I think that's a goal for all of us: To figure out who we are and where we fit in best. Where can I best unfold? For me, it's becoming more and more clear that the priesthood is where God wants me.

For Father Bob Couto, the decision came at age 44 and he was ordained at age 49:

> If you have this insatiable hunger... desire... thirst to help others come to know God, and you can't satisfy the hunger, God is calling you. I urge those considering the priesthood to meet God face to face in the everyday circum-

stances of life. I urge them to pray in earnest and to listen to their hearts and not to society. Discern. Seek encouragement and affirmation. Surrender to God and allow God to lead. The reward is the most precious gift one could ever ask for.

God will never force anyone to become a priest. God only asks, and you are free to say yes or no. The vocation process is a mystery. The priesthood is a mystery. The process of discerning whether or not you have a vocation is a mystery. In the end, it is always your decision, your free choice as to whether or not you want to enter into this mystery.

"I have chosen to be a prayerful, celibate and obedient priest," says Father Joseph Gatto. "Because I am a priest, I am a witness to how God's holiness penetrates people's lives. It affords me the freedom to be present at very unique moments of grace in people's lives during the Eucharist, in Reconciliation, at the Anointing of the Sick, at marriages, at funerals and at baptisms. When I cry, or when I am upset, or when I have to challenge people, I know that God has somehow specifically asked me to be present in those moments. That's what enamored me with priesthood and that's what nourishes me as a priest. I have the privilege of being present when God touches the world. I guess it's being sacramental. Sacramental is not just the seven Sacraments. Being sacramental is knowing that somehow, some way, by God's mysterious grace the incarnation is continuing. As a priest, I have chosen to participate in that mystery."

If you felt God calling you to make that choice, what would you say? Could you ever become a Catholic priest?

Chapter Notes

"In every situation, his task is to show God to man...": Pope John Paul II, "Letter to Priests for Holy Thursday 1996," L'Osservatore Romano, March 27, 1996.

"Recent studies show that men most interested...": Jerry Filteau, "New Study Finds Catholic Youth Interested in Church Vocations," Catholic News Service, May 23, 1997.

In a study of priests ordained ten to thirty years...: Grace Under Pressure, pp. 111-115.

Afterword

Christopher Duquin and his mother Lorene Duquin begin and end their fascinating book with a haunting question: "Could you ever become a Catholic priest?" This very question is rooted in yet an even more basic question, which every person must ask: "What is God asking of me?" As Pope John Paul II keeps telling us, every human person has been created by God for a very specific and unique "project" or purpose. When, through prayer and reflection, each of us comes to understand what God is asking and, through grace, accepts His will, we discover a profound sense of purpose and experience genuine inner peace.

Although all the People of God share in the common priesthood of Christ through the Sacrament of Baptism, God wills that some share in the ministerial priesthood of Christ through the Sacrament of Holy Orders. The vocation to the priesthood is necessary because there can be no Church without the Eucharist and there can be no Eucharist without the ordained priest.

There is no doubt that God is calling men — young and not so young — to serve as ordained priests. In the aftermath of recent World Youth Days in Denver, Manila and Paris, greater enthusiasm and interest have arisen regarding vocations to both the priesthood and consecrated life. Moreover, recent research has confirmed that those young people who are already involved in the Church are more likely to accept a vocation to serve as a priest, sister or brother.

Through their readable and informative work, Christopher Duquin and his mother Lorene have outlined for all of us a number of questions, issues and concerns surrounding the vocation to the priesthood. Even more, they have provided for those seriously considering that vocation a private and personal way to explore these very issues, questions and concerns.

The Year 1998 marks the third and final year of *Future Full of Hope: A National Strategy for Vocations to the Priesthood and Religious Life in the Dioceses and Archdioceses of the United States.* As the second in a three-year preparation for the two thousandth anniversary of Christ's Incarnation and Birth, the Year 1998 also is dedicated to the Holy Spirit and His sanctifying presence within the Community of Christ's disciples. How providential that this readable and positive overview of the process connected with discerning a vocation to the priesthood is being published in 1998. I see it as another confirming sign reminding us that the Holy Spirit is insistently asking many among us: "Could you ever become a Catholic priest?" and is empowering them to say in response: "Here I am! Form me in the image of Christ, Head and Shepherd of the Church, for the glory of God and the salvation of His people."

"Could you ever become a Catholic priest?" This readable and positive book will help many to say "Yes" and in no small way will contribute to a "Future Full of Hope."

Most Reverend Paul S. Loverde, STL, JCL
Bishop of Ogdensburg

For Additional
Information

PRINTED RESOURCES

Vocation Resource Catalogue
National Coalition for Church Vocations
5420 South Cornell Avenue, #105
Chicago, Illinois 60615
Phone: (800) 671-NCCV

The Vocation Resource Catalogue features books, videos, magazines and other materials designed to assist in vocation awareness and discernment.

A Guide to Religious Ministries for Catholic Men and Women
Catholic News Publishing Company
210 North Avenue
New Rochelle, New York 10801
Phone: (914) 632-1220

This guide includes a helpful introduction to various types of vocations in the Church today with an extensive listing of Diocesan Vocation Directors and Religious Communities of Priests, Brothers and Sisters in the United States.

ASSOCIATIONS

National Conference of Diocesan Vocation Directors
P.O. Box 1570
Little River, South Carolina 29566
Phone: (803) 280-7191
This organization can supply the names and addresses of
Vocation Directors in each diocese.

National Religious Vocation Conference
5420 South Cornell Avenue, #105
Chicago, Illinois 60615
Phone: (773) 363-5454
This organization can supply the names and addresses of
Vocation Directors in various religious communities.

USA/Canada Council of Serra International
Suite 1210
65 East Walker Place
Chicago, Illinois 60601
Phone: (800) 488-4008
e-mail: SerraUS@aol.com
web site: SerraUS.org
This organization can supply the names and addresses of
Vocation Directors in dioceses and religious communities through-
out the United States and Canada.

VOCATION MAGAZINES

• **Vision** magazine features informative articles on priesthood
and religious life, prayer, and discernment along with advertisement.
This magazine is available through Vocation offices. It is pub-
lished by:
Claretian Publications
205 West Monroe Street
Chicago, Illinois 60606
Phone: (800) 328-6515

• **Vocations and Prayer** magazine features articles on religious life, trends in vocation ministry, discernment, and prayer. It is published quarterly by:
The Rogationist Fathers
9815 Columbus Avenue
North Hills, California 91343
Phone: (818) 895-8924

SEMINARIES SPECIALIZING IN LATE VOCATIONS

The following seminaries specialize in the formation of men who recognize a call to the priesthood later in life:

Holy Apostles College and Seminary
33 Prospect Hill Road
Cromwell, Connecticut 06416
Phone: (860) 632-3030

Sacred Heart School of Theology
7335 South Highway 100
P.O. Box 429
Hales Corners, Wisconsin 53130
Phone: (414) 425-8300

Pope John XXIII National Seminary
558 South Avenue
Weston, Massachusetts 02193-2699
Phone: (617) 899-5500

Mater Dei Institute
East 405 Sinto
Spokane, Washington 99202
Phone: (509) 328-8332

WEB SITES

To find vocation information on the internet, enter key words into your search engine. For example, you can begin with a broad search and get thousands of matches by entering the words "religious communities."

To refine your search, you can enter an exact name, i.e. "Oblates," or "Redemptorists" or "Benedictines" or "Paulists."

If you're looking for general information about vocations to the diocesan priesthood or general information about religious life, most dioceses have a vocation link on their web pages. You can enter the words "Diocese of" or "Archdiocese of" to access a list of diocesan web sites.

* * * * * *

This book was designed and published by ST PAULS / ALBA HOUSE, the publishing arm of the Society of St. Paul, an international religious congregation of priests and brothers dedicated to serving the Church through the communications media. For more information regarding this and associated ministries of the Pauline Family of Congregations, write to the Vocation Director, Society of St. Paul, 7050 Pinehurst, Dearborn, Michigan 48126 or check the internet site, WWW.ALBAHOUSE.ORG